NINE LIVES

NINE LIVES

A CHEF'S JOURNEY FROM CHAOS TO CONTROL

BRANDON BALTZLEY

GOTHAM
BOOKS

GOTHAM BOOKS
Published by the Penguin Group
Penguin Group (USA) Inc., 375 Hudson Street,
New York, New York 10014, USA

USA | Canada | UK | Ireland | Australia | New Zealand | India | South Africa | China
Penguin Books Ltd, Registered Offices: 80 Strand, London WC2R 0RL, England
For more information about the Penguin Group visit penguin.com.

LIBRARY OF CONGRESS CATALOGING-IN-PUBLICATION DATA
Baltzley, Brandon.
    Nine lives : a chef's journey from chaos to control / Brandon Baltzley.
    pages   cm.

ISBN 978-1-592-40791-0 (hardback)
    1. Baltzley, Brandon. 2. Cooks—United States—Biography. 3. Drummers
(Musicians)—United States—Biography. 4. Addicts—United States—Biography.
I. Title.
    TX649.B35A3   2013
    641.5029—dc23   2012050511

Printed in the United States of America
10 9 8 7 6 5 4 3 2 1

While the author has made every effort to provide accurate telephone numbers, Internet addresses, and other contact information at the time of publication, neither the
publisher nor the author assumes any responsibility for errors or for changes that occur
after publication. Further, the publisher does not have any control over and does not
assume any responsibility for author or third-party websites or their content.

Penguin is committed to publishing works of quality and integrity.
In that spirit, we are proud to offer this book to our readers;
however, the story, the experiences, and the words
are the author's alone.

To the memory of Thomas Eason; for Thomas's daughter, Amber Baltzley; Chris Genoversa; and the Hansen family

8453

Disclaimer: This work recounts past events to the best of my ability. Some names have been changed to protect the privacy of those most likely needing it as a result of being caught up in this story. Some events may seem vague. I assure you any ambiguity is the result of a series of punishing years my body and mind endured and not a feeble attempt to save face. That ship has sailed . . . and apparently established a fairly regular trade route.

NINE LIVES

PROLOGUE

On May 17, 2011, I thought my life was over. I was just twenty-six years old, but I had a job that most people only dream about. After years of working in Michelin-starred restaurants in New York and Chicago, I was about to be the opening chef at a spot on Michigan Avenue that everyone seemed to be talking about. People called me a prodigy. They called me the Salvador Dali of cooking. Food blogs followed my every move. But I couldn't do it. I was only twenty-six years old, but I'd been addicted to alcohol and cocaine for more than six years. I'd tried and failed to get clean tons of times, but addiction had me in a choke hold. This time, it seemed like it had fucked me over for good. And not only that, but I had let the world watch. The *Chicago Tribune* was running a profile on me, so there was a reporter literally sitting next to me as I let it all fall, leaving my dream job and heading for rehab.

Sitting in the car on the way to rehab that day, the reporter asked me a question I'd gotten countless times before. When did I start cooking? Had I always known I wanted to be a chef? I thought back, scanning the endless stream of kitchen jobs I'd had since I was a teenager, and started to talk about washing dishes at the Cool Moose Café in Jacksonville, Florida, when I was a teenager, about how that had turned into a line cook job, which had taken me to Stella's Piano Café and onward.

But then I stopped. That wasn't the answer. The answer was the Whistle Stop Café.

It was the mid-1990s, and I was nine years old when my mother bought the bar kitchen in the back of the Jerviston Junction, a Jacksonville gay bar. It wasn't much—probably twelve feet by twenty feet—and the kitchen was so small she had to keep the cash register outside the door in plain sight of any of the patrons. And it wasn't high cuisine—there was a cold station with Boar's Head lunch meat for sandwiches, and one tiny oven where she made Delmonico steaks (sold for ten dollars with a salad and a baked potato). And every morning, she started out making a huge batch of turkey corn chowder, the "house soup," which she kept simmering in a crock pot on the stainless steel counter all day long.

Even though it wasn't extravagant, the Whistle Stop Café was entirely my mother's and something that she could be proud of when there wasn't much else good happening in life. My mom went through plenty of rough patches in her life, not terribly different from the one I was going through myself, sitting in that cab on my way to rehab in 2011. But she also knew how to reinvent herself. She wasn't trained as a chef, but even at nine years old, I could see that she was skilled. And, more important, that she was at peace in the kitchen, producing simple food and keeping people nourished and happy.

Opening a restaurant—even a little one like the Whistle Stop Café—wasn't easy as a single mom, and so she ended up having to bring me to the kitchen most days after school. I was a hyper kid, not one to be content reading or watching her cook, so after about a week of me running around making trouble, she grabbed a child-size apron, a step stool, and a knife about the size of my head at the time, and put me to work cutting corn off the cob to go in the turkey chowder. Cooking held my attention like nothing ever had before, and from the first moment, I was hooked.

I credit my mother not only with putting that first knife in my hand, but also with helping me to think about food differently from most other kids. She taught me to scramble eggs when I was five—more out of necessity for herself than anything else. Knowing how to scramble eggs meant that I could help myself when I was hungry, and she didn't have to be around to make sure I got fed. But instead of just showing me the basics, she also gave me the run of her spice cabinet, and instilled in me the joy of experimentation. I could go through a full dozen eggs in an afternoon after school—throwing things together, tasting them, and then trying again with a different combination of flavors.

When I was around nine years old, I had my first real dining experience. My mother took me to a restaurant that served escargots, and she ordered them for me without telling me what they were. Of course, I fucking loved them. They were so good that, in my mind, I couldn't understand how they wouldn't be on every menu at every restaurant, and I couldn't wait to eat out again. My mom loves telling me about how the next time we were on a road trip, ordering in a McDonald's drive-through, she asked me what I wanted and I replied, "Garlic snails!"

By the time I was in middle school, my mom no longer owned the Whistle Stop, and I wasn't much interested in hanging around making turkey chowder with her. I'd started spending most of my time with a group of four guys: Michael, Scott, Trey, and James. We were like most kids hanging out in Jacksonville those days—we skateboarded, we listened to punk rock and hardcore, went to shows, and liked to get into trouble. We spent most of our weekday afternoons hanging out in Trey's garage, practicing covers for our punk-noise band, but on weekends, we were always at my house. We would stay up to the crack of dawn, maybe sleeping for only an hour, after inevitably sneaking the occasional beer and cigarette from my mother's stash over the course of the night. When the sun rose, we would skate over the Cedar River Bridge, into strip mall parking lots or closed banks.

By noon, we'd always make it back to my house. The summer sun in northern Florida is not kind, and by then we'd be exhausted from our night out. But more importantly, there was always one thing we could count on: food. And I'm not just talking about frozen pizzas.

Even when my mom wasn't working in a kitchen, she was always cooking something. It could be one hundred degrees out and we could come home to a beer-braised pork shoulder. Other times, my mom would make steaks for six different kids, covering the meat in sautéed mushrooms and taking temps for every kid's preference. She had an old, worn-out copy of *The Joy of Cooking*, and an ever-expanding rotation of teenage boys plowing through her kitchen, sunburnt and tired and ready to dig into any food she put in front of them.

There were hard times in my childhood, but I never went hungry, and neither did any of the friends I grew up with. We all learned to eat at my mom's kitchen table, and even though none of us are really close anymore, it's still something that connects us, and something that we talk about every time we're in touch.

I wouldn't be a cook today had my mom not showed me the true beauty of cooking for others and sharing the pure pleasure of food with the people you love. She's the one who filled my belly as a child, and the one who put the first knife in my hand. But more than anything else, it was the look on her face as she cooked at the Whistle Stop Café that came back to me that morning in the cab on my way to rehab. It was as serene as I have ever seen my mother. Tranquil. She was at peace with her surroundings, and nothing outside of the moment could ruin that.

I didn't last terribly long in rehab that May. But I did get myself sober. I've been far more in control of my life and my impulses since then and have embarked on so many new projects that it's hard to fathom that it's been only a couple of years. Most important, I founded a culinary collective called Crux. The word means a pivotal point, a puzzling problem, the most important part. More than a restaurant idea, it's a philosophy, an ever-evolving concept that's now made its mark in cities and on farms and in restaurants all over the world.

I know now that Crux wouldn't have been possible if I hadn't had my mother guiding me by her example. The food at the Whistle Stop Café was no different from what we ate at home, or what she made for family and friends, which is exactly what we aspire to at Crux. Through it all, there was a spirit of adventure, of experimentation, and most important, of nourishing and providing for the people she felt understood her best. She was able to make something of herself by doing what gave her pure freedom, and above all else, she taught me to do the same. And she never gave up, reinventing herself over and over again, opening doors where there didn't even seem to be a window.

It seemed impossible at the time, but sitting in that dismal cab, talking to the reporter about my past, I was also laying out a plan for my future. I didn't know it then, but I was about to have my own Whistle Stop Café.

In some ways, my life did end on May 17, 2011. But just as quickly, another one started. This is the story of how it happened.

CHAPTER ONE

I arrived in DC on an Amtrak train from Savannah, Georgia, just after my twenty-first birthday. I was fresh out of my first stint in rehab—two weeks in the South Carolina woods—and looking for work. In a day, I had my first job as chef de cuisine of a major restaurant. Two weeks later, I had my first hit of crack. It's safe to say I wasn't prepared for either.

I'd been to DC only once before, to play a show with my metal band Kylesa, in the middle of a year-long tour during which every city became the same. So I had no idea what I was getting into, on any level. There wasn't a whole lot of planning going on in my life at that point. I moved all the time, following jobs and bands and drugs and girls.

This time, it was a girl.

I met Chloe at Cha Bella in Savannah, where she was a server and I was the sous chef. She was a theatre major at the Savannah College of Art and Design, a fiery, obnoxious ball of energy with a crazy temper, who used to annoy the hell out of my friends. We'd been together for nine months, which was an eternity to me at the time.

Our relationship was fierce and intense and you didn't need to be a shrink to tell that it was destructive as hell for both of us. We partied hard together in Savannah, getting blitzed after our shifts and then getting into these epic fights that woke up our entire neighborhood. Chloe was a mean, angry drunk, and I guess I gave her every reason to be. We'd get wasted, she'd get paranoid about something I'd done, I'd lie to her, she'd start hitting me, and I'd laugh. It made everything worse, of course, but when I was drunk and high, it was the funniest thing I'd ever seen—this little peanut just kicking and screaming her head off.

Chloe was two months shy of graduating from the Savannah College of Art and Design and wanted to move back home to Falls Church, Virginia, a quiet suburb about twenty minutes outside of DC. I knew in my gut that she loved me more than I loved her, which can only lead to disaster, but I was going nowhere fast in Savannah and had to get the hell out of Dodge.

Chloe's parents had agreed to let us stay with them while we got settled, an arrangement that grew a little more complicated when it turned out that Chloe had to stay in Savannah for an extra month to finish her finals: If I landed one of the jobs I had interviews lined up for in DC, it would be just me and her folks for a while. Her parents were having their house renovated and were living in a condo that had two separate entrances, which was the only reason I even considered it. But just the three of us under one roof still gave me pause.

I guess you could say I wasn't exactly what Chloe's parents had in mind for their daughter. To be more fair: They fucking hated me. To start, both of her parents worked for the government, and her dad was, swear to God, an actual ex–CIA agent. We're talking total *Meet the Parents* shit.

Plus, there was a reason for Chloe's tough-as-nails bravado. Chloe was in high school when she contracted breast cancer for the first time. She gave it a good beating with chemo and a macrobiotic diet and was cancer-free by the time I met her. But if there was ever a reason for parents to be protective, that was it.

I'm still a little sketchy on how much Chloe's parents knew about her drug use, but they definitely knew about mine. After a particularly bad bender in Savannah, I'd promised Chloe that I'd go to rehab, but I could only come up with half the cash for it. Chloe loved me and wanted to make it work, and her parents loved her and wanted her to be happy, so they paid the other half.

When I got off the train at Union Station that May afternoon, the pressure was already on. I was just barely sober, had fucking Robert De Niro with a lie detector literally invested in that sobriety, a tenuous living situation, a relationship hanging in the balance, and a job interview at Restaurant Nora.

I'd found the job ad—for a sous chef position—on the Internet and threw in my resume back in Savannah, not knowing much about the restaurant or if I'd be a good fit for it. But I'd been working in kitchens since I was nine years old, which, I was pretty sure at the time, made me the shit. And it's not like I was just frying eggs at the neighborhood diner. I'd risen through the ranks quickly in Jacksonville and Savannah, cooking at what were unequivocally the nicest restaurants in town.

What I didn't realize then was that the town made a pretty big difference.

I got off the train and took a quick ride on the Red Line to Dupont Circle, then checked the slip of paper where I'd written down the address: 2132 Florida Avenue NW. Well. That was an auspicious beginning. I'd come a long way from Jacksonville just to be back in Florida.

Fortunately, the leafy streets and brownstones were a little different from the palm trees and busted-up trailer parks I was used to. And Nora itself wasn't like anywhere I'd ever worked before, either. It's in this beautiful, hundred-year-old building right off Dupont Circle, and there were politicians and lobbyists buzzing around like it was a fucking honeycomb. I walked into the main dining room—all polished wood and old Amish quilts hanging everywhere—and could literally see deals being made in front of me. The political system at work, right where I had a job interview.

I headed into the kitchen and was met by a middle-aged woman, maybe fifty or so, with shaggy brown hair and a thick German accent. It was the owner, Nora Pouillon, and she was a force of nature. Right away, she started talking, telling me about herself and her cooking philosophy.

She was born in Austria, married a French dude and kept his name, even though they were long separated and she'd been with her partner, Steven, who also owned the restaurant with her, for years. She came to America in the 1960s and couldn't believe all the processed food people were eating, and she made it her mission to try to change that. There wasn't even butter on her menu—everything was in oils. Everything was healthy.

Restaurant Nora had been around for more than twenty-five years doing local, sustainable, organic food long before anyone thought it was cool. In 1999, almost seven years before my interview—Nora became the first fully certified organic restaurant in America, which means that 95 percent of everything served there was produced by organic farmers. (The rest, which she imported, were mostly tropical ingredients like limes, coconuts, and mangoes.) Only three other restaurants in the country have been certified since then. Everyone talks about Chez Panisse, but Nora is like the East Coast version—a total pioneer.

Nora paused and looked me up and down: "No chef's whites?"

"Shit," I said, looking down at the suit I was wearing. "I didn't know I had to stage for a sous chef job."

"Sweetie, this isn't for a sous chef job. I need a chef de cuisine." She threw me a chef's coat and showed me where to change. "And you're cooking the specials for the night. I need one appetizer and one entrée."

Staging is the linchpin of the interview process for chefs—it's like an audition and usually involves cooking a sample meal for the chef. But this was an unusual twist. The fact that Nora was offering my dishes as the specials for the night meant that I wasn't just cooking for her: I'd be working the line. This meant that, no matter what, customers were going to be eating my food that night.

For the appetizer, I decided to make a crab cake with lobster bubbles and a fennel orange salad on the side. In retrospect, I had some real balls, making a crab cake ten minutes from the Maryland border. It may even have been what got me the job—the total lack of fear. But to be honest, I was so naïve that it hadn't even crossed my mind. A simple crab cake was one of the first things I ever learned how to cook, when I was growing up in Jacksonville. There are a million and a half ways to make one, but I'd played around with the fennel, orange, crab profile before, and I felt good about it, so that's what I went with.

Nora had some rib eye that she wanted me to use in the entrée, so I paired it with a red onion marmalade, pomme fondant, and a bordelaise sauce with steamed greens on the side. As with the crab, I'd picked up some of the technique at Bistro Aix in Jacksonville, one of the first places I ever worked, and tweaked it to fit Nora's menu.

In addition to being a chef, I'm also a drummer—a pretty serious one. I toured the country as the drummer in Kylesa, a popular metal band out of Savannah. I may have been green in the kitchen, especially in one as esteemed as Nora's, but there was one thing I knew. Cooking is like pounding out a goddamn drumbeat. You keep the same things going over and over again, and fix them every place you go. I've probably made those two dishes at every restaurant I've ever worked at. Same beat, different twist every time.

Halfway through service, Nora pulled me off the line and took me outside to this amazing little garden in the back of the restaurant. We sat on a wooden swing chair and she asked me about my tattoos. She was a total health nut—to her, the body was sacred, and she didn't understand what I was doing to mine. I couldn't help but laugh. If only she knew that tattoos were pretty much the least offensive things I'd done to my body. Instead, I told her that I'd think about organic ink.

She reached into the pocket of her chef's pants and pulled out a copy of my resume. I'd been so proud of it, sending it off in Savannah. But sitting in this garden, next to this culinary legend, it suddenly seemed ridiculous. Bistro Aix, Cha Bella. What the hell were they, compared to this kind of restaurant?

"So, you have no formal training? No culinary school?"

My stomach dropped: "No, ma'am. But I've been working in kitchens since I was nine years old. I know food."

She nodded, but I couldn't read her face.

"I want this," I said, and suddenly I knew I really did. "I'll work hard for you."

"Okay, sweetie," she said, putting my resume down, "I'm going to be honest. I thought your food was excellent. Healthy, fresh, seasonal. It's exactly what I want for my restaurant."

I grinned, and let my chest puff out again a little bit. She loved my food. I knew she would, and she did.

"But are you sure you're ready for this? Running a full kitchen?"

I paused, and Nora laughed.

"I guess no one's really ever ready for that. Won't know until you try. Now let's make sure I can afford you. What were you thinking in terms of salary?"

Jesus. No one had ever asked me that before. I'd been

scraping by for so long—since I was fifteen years old, really—and I had no idea what money meant in a city like DC.

"Forty thousand?" I guessed, thinking I was aiming high.

Nora laughed. "Oh, that won't do at all. This is Washington. No one can live on forty thousand dollars a year here. I'll give you sixty-five thousand, plus benefits, of course."

My mind was blown. I'd come in that morning thinking I'd be doing the same thing I always had. Now I was going to be chef de cuisine. Second in command. For more money than I could even fathom. I thought back to Nora's question. Was I ready for this? Probably not.

But this wasn't an opportunity you passed up. I didn't even hesitate—I just said yes, and went back to Chloe's parents' house feeling like the luckiest fucking bastard in the world.

I still had a swagger in my step the next day when I showed up to work for the first time. I'd need to lose it, quickly.

First on the agenda was a menu meeting with Nora and the two chefs that I'd have the most contact with: Yoshi, the chef de cuisine at Nora's other restaurant, Asia Nora, and Carlos, who would be my sous chef.

Nora told me that Yoshi would mostly be the one training me, and I was grateful for that. She was cool—this beautiful Japanese woman maybe in her mid-thirties who was married to some old guy I think Nora hooked her up with. I started to get the feeling that Nora's wings were pretty big, and she just collected people she wanted under them.

Yoshi knew her shit, and didn't seem to care about my age. Right away, we started talking food, and I could tell we'd see eye to eye. She was doing really nice things at Asia Nora—

a lot of seafood, organic duck breasts, pork loins, dumplings. Simple fusion food with spot-on flavor profiles.

Carlos was another story. I'd met him when I was staging the night before, and he was good. I mean really, really good. His flavors were perfect, and his plating was just impeccable—every dish was like a goddamn Michelangelo. Years later, even after cooking at many of the finest restaurants in the country, I still think his work was some of the best I've ever seen.

Maybe even more important, though: The dude was all business. He got there early, stayed there late, and had a focus like nothing I'd ever seen before. He told me that he ran eight miles before work every day and after the long, sweaty shift, when the rest of the kitchen was cracking open beers or bottles of wine, he had just one, tall glass of orange juice.

The problem was that Carlos had been working at Nora's for four years at twenty dollars an hour, and I know he must have been pissed as hell that she'd hired some twenty-one-year-old kid above him instead of considering him for the job. He was a total professional, and he didn't say anything to me directly. But I could see it in his eyes that first morning when we were about to start the menu meeting. He just looked me up and down hard, nodded once, and then silently put his head down. I tense up just thinking about that fucking stare, even now. To this day, I never grasped why he didn't originally get the job.

Nora started off the menu meeting talking about the product that we'd gotten in that morning. Fresh, seasonal ingredients were everything to her, and always determined what we'd be making for specials.

Most chefs who buy locally even today use a 100-mile rule, so that everything served has to be grown within that radius. Nora cut hers down to around forty-five miles, and took it a step further—she tried, whenever possible, to buy only from Amish farmers from just over the Pennsylvania border. They'd show up every morning to make deliveries in their full garb—suspenders, broad-brimmed black hats, the whole nine yards—and it was the most incredible variety of produce I'd ever seen. It was as if the big walk-in reinvented itself every morning with perfect, fresh, overflowing bounty.

That day, Nora was all worked up about some green she'd been waiting on for weeks:

"The ramps are here!" she announced, like it was Christmas morning and she was in a room full of Amish elves.

Ramps? The only ramps I'd ever heard of were for skateboards or wheelchairs and we sure as shit didn't have either of those in the kitchen.

"Ramps?" I asked out loud, wondering if I just couldn't understand her thick accent.

"Yah," she said, "ramps. What should we do with them?"

Carlos and Yoshi were in on the game, too, nodding and tossing around ideas:

"Fresh linguini, maybe?"

"A risotto?"

Nora looked straight at me: "What do you think, Chef? What would you do with them?"

Fuck.

"Uh. Could I taste one?" I asked. "Just for inspiration?"

Nora nodded and trotted off to the walk-in, returning

with what looked like a bunch of wild leeks. I love them now, and know that they're available only a few weeks out of the year, which I guess explains why Nora was so pumped. But in Georgia and South Carolina, they grow like grass, and that's how we treated them.

"Oh!" I said, recognizing them immediately. "Down south we just call those weeds."

Nora and Yoshi looked at me like I was slow, and Carlos just narrowed his eyes. I was off to quite a start. The rest of that week was a learning curve the size of Mount Everest.

First of all, Nora's kitchen was like working in the United Nations, which, coming from white-bread Savannah, seemed insane. There must've been thirty people working in the kitchen at any given time, and I was literally the only native English speaker.

The daytime prep cooks were Vietnamese, and they never said a word to me. They were the first ones to get there during the day, so every morning when I'd roll in around ten, the kitchen would smell like fish sauce and coriander and there'd be an incredibly fresh, homemade pho loaded with ginger and cilantro and beef tendons waiting for me for breakfast.

Like Yoshi, the butcher was also Japanese, this amazing, total Mr. Miyagi type who seemed to have the cure for any ailment. He was always steeping teas with herbs and roots and serving them to me, and then would teach me, slowly as I drank them, about butchering and handling meat.

Carlos was Cuban, and a Mexican guy named Ramon headed up the back kitchen, which did all of the catering and private parties. Nora had told me that he had a problem with alcohol and wasn't allowed to drink at work, but he'd been at Nora for decades, and the dude could pump out some major food. And, as in most big-city kitchens, the rest of the line cooks were pretty much all Spanish speakers, too—Cubans, Mexicans, Ecuadorians, you name it.

The great thing about having such an international kitchen was that Nora was totally open to different ethnic influences on her food. As long as it was fresh and organic, she was game. Yoshi started teaching me about raw fish, and we were doing crudos and sashimis. And the next night, we'd have a lamb dish with hummus and garam masala. As long as the flavor profiles were right, we didn't have to pigeonhole ourselves.

But the language barriers were deep, and I was the odd man out. Right away, Carlos and I started switching off every night working the line—he'd work one night and I'd plate, and then we'd swap the next night. I knew I could cook—I was a beast on the line. Just kept my head down and got it done. But the line spoke Spanish like Carlos, and I didn't know Spanish, so I didn't know the line calls, and I was screwed. The line knew English, but would call back in Spanish. I guess it was their way of reminding me where I was on a daily basis.

Not only was I the only English speaker in the kitchen, but I was also the youngest, by at least ten years. I've always hung out with older people—as an only child, I was used to being around my mom and her friends, and I started playing in bands regularly as a teenager with guys in their twenties and thirties. But hanging out, playing music—that was worlds apart from being a boss.

Now I was managing an average of nine people every

night—three cooks on the hot line, three on cold, two on pastry, and, of course, Carlos. On busy nights, we were turning three hundred covers, which is insane. And for the first time, I had to be the one worried about whether people were in the right places, whether plates were coming out on time, making sure that food was covered properly, stored the right way, things like that.

I'd mostly kept to myself that first week, keeping my head down and focusing on my cooking, then cleaning up and catching a cab back to Falls Church late at night. The situation with the kitchen staff was awkward enough as it was—I figured they didn't need me lurking around afterward, too. So when Saturday rolled around, I was surprised to see someone lingering in the kitchen after service, waiting for me.

It was Nora's assistant—this cute, curly-haired little lady named Jessica. She must have been twenty-five or twenty-six then—five years older than I was, but compared to everyone else, that felt close enough.

"Where're you headed?" she asked.

"Just home, I guess," I said, looking at my watch. "Shit, I missed the last train again."

For a big city, DC's subway system is ridiculous. The last trains ran at twelve thirty in the morning—right when I was usually getting off work—so if I missed it, it was at least a forty-dollar cab ride back to Falls Church.

"Well, if you have to take a cab home anyway, you might as well come out with us." She jerked her head to the door, where her girlfriend was waiting. "Come on, it'll be fun. We're going to check out the chicks at this new bar in Dupont."

I hesitated. I've done some shady things in my day, but I've never really been much for titty bars. I'm not sure I'd even been to one before that first week in DC.

And I was straight out of rehab. This was exactly the kind of situation I'd promised myself I'd avoid.

Even more important, I hadn't gotten a paycheck yet. The restaurant was closed on Sundays, so payday was Monday, and until then, I didn't have a pot to piss in.

"I would," I told her, "but I'm broke. Until Monday, I'm running on empty."

"Bullshit excuse," she said. "I'll front you the cash."

"No way, dude. I'm not making you do that."

"You're not making me do anything. You're the first guy from work that's ever seemed down to hang out. Consider it a favor to me."

"Well . . ."

"Oh, just come on. You made it through a week—at least let's toast to that. Besides, we're only going for one drink."

Famous last words.

Twelve hours later, I woke up on a couch in Jessica's apartment, reeking of whiskey and vomit, honestly more hungover than I ever remember being before. I was sweating and shaking, and my tongue felt like it was covered in sawdust. Just trying to lift my head took an eternity—and when I did, I wished I hadn't. Next to me, on Jessica's brand-new hardwood floor, was a bong rolling around sideways in a chunky pile of my vomit.

Pieces of the night started coming back to me in vague splinters. There were shots—that much I was sure of. A lap dance. Then more shots. Eventually, we'd left the strip club and gone to another bar. Maybe two? I think Jessica and her girlfriend had picked up a chick at one of them, and she'd come back to the house with us to smoke.

I coughed, and my throat burned with the remnants of stale resin.

My stomach heaved again.

A wave of embarrassment mingled with the nausea, and I felt as stupid as I did sick. Jessica was the one person who seemed to like me at work, and I'd literally just puked all over her home.

I didn't know where she had gone, and I wanted to get out of there as soon as possible, so I managed eventually to get myself up. I found some paper towels, cleaned up the puke as best I could, and then stashed them where I hoped she wouldn't see. I left before Jessica was up and moving, and got myself home.

I slept off my hangover all day Sunday, went back to work on Monday, and the next night went right back to the same bar. This time, I was alone. Jessica and I stayed cool, and we never mentioned that night again. But we definitely didn't keep hanging out like that, either. In one dumb-ass move, I'd lost my only comrade there.

I wish I could say it was just a little lapse—some drinking, a few bong hits, and a bad stomachache the next morning. But for an addict, that's all it takes. I'd worked my ass off to get clean in South Carolina, and after a single night, it was all back in my system—not just the alcohol and weed but, most important, this intangible taste for partying. The feeling that what I was doing wasn't really so wrong. And now I also had money in my pocket—more than I'd ever made at one time before.

I was a few drinks in that Tuesday night when I knew what I really wanted was some coke. I had been using for about three years now and excessive alcohol abuse would always bring out the craving in me. I looked around, trying to figure out where I could score some, when one of the strippers, fresh off her shift, came over and sat next to me. She was Latina, Cuban probably, and just absolutely gorgeous. Without a doubt the hottest girl in the strip club.

It was like all my teenage wet dreams finally coming true.

I asked her if she knew where I could get coke, and she whipped out a bag like it was a pack of gum. I took a deep breath and felt a quick flicker of guilt as I thought about rehab, about all the guys who'd worked with me. About my pledges never to do this again.

And about Chloe. I hadn't told her what had happened Saturday night. Her parents were away, so they didn't know that I hadn't come home, and I didn't volunteer it. I knew she'd be disappointed in me. But God, I wanted it. And whatever, I thought. She was probably doing it, too, down in Savannah without me. The stripper took my hand and pulled me into the bathroom and we did a line. And then another one. It felt as good as I remembered.

The supply was dwindling quickly when she said she knew a club nearby.

"Want to get out of here?"

Despite my coke habit, I'd never been that into clubs. I'm

usually much happier in a dive, punk bar, sitting in the corner smoking and listening to Merle Haggard, than waiting outside next to a red velvet rope. But I'd never felt more like a baller than I did that night. I was high as a kite, had what I thought was serious money in my pocket to burn, and had just been legitimately picked up by a stripper.

Fuck, yeah, I wanted to get out of there.

The rest of the night was a blur of drugs and sex. We mostly wandered around the city, scoring a few more bags of coke from bouncers we met, and ended up in a $350 hotel room. I do remember that the girl had this giant wad of hundred-dollar bills with her from her tips that evening, stuffed into a Crown Royal bag. She must have been carrying ten grand around with her all night.

The stripper left around eight the next morning, and I stayed in the room for a while, freaking out like a mental patient. Grinding my teeth and shivering and hoping like hell that I didn't have an STD. The sun was streaming in the windows and it was just scorching my eyes until I felt like I was going blind. I hadn't slept at all.

In a haze, I remembered that not only was I supposed to go to work, but I also had a special dinner with Nora, Yoshi, and their husbands that night. I tried to think of any way I could clean myself up and get my act together in time to do it, but it just didn't seem possible. I sent a text to Nora, telling her I was sick, knowing that I was using up a good excuse really early on and I couldn't do it every time I got wasted.

I think part of me wished she would see through it. That she'd yell at me, or fire me, or do something to make me feel less bad about screwing up this incredible opportunity. But she just wrote back that she was sorry, and asked if I needed anything.

Sheepishly, I took a cab back to my girlfriend's parents' house, full of shame and regret and a million other vile things. Vowing to myself that I'd never do it again. It was the drugs that made me cheat, the drugs that made me miss this special dinner, the drugs that made me fail the people who'd taken me into their home. I was told upon invitation that Nora doesn't invite her staff into her home for dinner very often and it was made very clear, the following day, that my no-show was taken as an offense, regardless of my excuse.

Yet the next night, I was back at the bar, looking for coke like there was a fucking magnet in my pocket, dragging me there.

The next few nights went the same way. I'd finish work at Nora at around twelve thirty, and immediately head over to the bars in Dupont to find drugs. Somehow, it became easy enough to justify to myself. Chloe's parents were still away, so there was no one to keep tabs on me. And since the only way home was a cab ride anyway, it didn't matter how late I stayed out. Eventually, I'd find my way back, sleep for a few hours, and then take the Metro back into town and start all over again the next day.

After a week or so of the same routine, I felt like the bars were starting to be a waste of time. I always went out alone, and there wasn't any reason to sit around drinking and waiting to find someone there that might have coke when I could go straight to the source—the streets.

I'd seen this kid hanging around Dupont who looked like he knew what he was doing. He was probably a few years older than me—a light-skinned black dude with an Afro and baggy pants who always had a skateboard with him. He was obviously an addict—I could tell from the look in his eyes and from the scabs all over his face, which so many addicts have from the paranoia or anxiety that drives them to pick and scratch at their skin far beyond merely popping a pimple.

I called the kid over and asked if he knew where I could get some coke.

Without saying anything, he wheeled away on his board and went to talk to this other guy, a few feet away, who was leaning against a mailbox. A few minutes later, he wheeled back and asked me for twenty dollars. I was confused—there's no way to get even a gram of coke for less than fifty dollars. But I was drunk already, and not really thinking straight. I handed him the cash, and when he came back, he was holding these two little green baggies with one solid rock in each.

What was happening?

Did this kid just buy me crack?

I was already a cokehead, but there's something about crack that, even to an addict, feels really . . . real. Crack is a purer form of cocaine. It's much stronger than coke and has an extreme addictive quality. You can drink and smoke weed and snort lines all you want. But somehow, until you're looking a crack rock in the face, it doesn't really feel that bad.

The kid dragged me into an alley, pulled out a pipe, and started showing me how to work it. The pipe is actually a glass tube with a little piece of Brillo pad that, when heated

with a flame, melts and keeps the rock in place while it pro-
duces the vapor you inhale. Skateboard set it up, then handed
me the pipe.

Fuck it, I thought, and inhaled deeply.

The smoke tasted sweet, almost sickly.

"Suck it down," Skateboard was saying. "Just keep it in
your lungs as long as you can."

I exhaled. And holy shit. Literally within seconds, I could
feel it, and it was just straight euphoria. It was like doing five
lines of coke at once, pulsing through every cell of my body.
My gums went numb, as if all the blood were running out of
them, and my heartbeat started echoing through my body.
Everything around me seemed to fade. I felt totally alive, like
I'd never felt before.

Five minutes later, the high had worn off, and all I could
think about was getting more. I'd seen my share of DARE
commercials as a kid, so I knew that crack was more addictive
even than straight coke, but nothing prepared me for that raw,
instantaneous craving. I needed it, badly, from the second the
first hit wore off.

And the next thing I knew, Skateboard and I had copped
$160 worth and were walking around the streets of DC,
smoking rock after rock. I didn't even make it home that
night. Just showed up at the beautiful fucking building that
was Nora's at ten A.M., haggard and dirty and crashing harder
than I ever had before.

One of the prep cooks was spooning out bowls of pho,
and my stomach turned at the smell of the hot, salty broth. I
beelined for the bathroom and emptied my guts into the toilet,

then straightened and looked at my pathetic reflection in the mirror. There were giant raccoon circles under my eyes, and my greasy hair was matted against the back of my neck. My skin felt clammy and my shirt was soaked with sweat.

The crack high was higher than anything I'd ever felt, but that meant the low was that much lower. I hated myself as I looked in the mirror, felt disgusted at the sight of my own face. I just wanted to curl up into a ball and erase the last twenty-four hours.

I splashed water on my face and willed myself to suck it up and get it together before the menu meeting.

Nora and Yoshi barely even glanced my way as they started going through ingredients, but I could tell that Carlos knew something was up. Looking at him sitting up straight and alert, ready with whatever Nora wanted from him, made my shame even worse. I slumped in my chair, and fought harder than I'd ever had to, just to keep my eyelids from closing.

I knew I wasn't going to make it through the night without a miracle. And as much as I didn't want to use it, I still had one in my pocket. After the menu meeting ended, I slunk back downstairs to the bathroom, reached for the pipe Skateboard had given me, and even though I knew in every cell of my broken body that it was wrong, I did drugs during work for the first time.

Feeling the crack pulse through my veins, jolting pure energy into my body—in that moment, it was as if it was the only thing keeping me alive. Just a few minutes before, a night on the line had seemed impossible, and then it wasn't anymore. I kept my head down, cooked my ass off, and when my shift ended, I was beyond fiending for another hit. I saw Skate-board waiting for me outside, and I was ready for more.

For the next couple of months, my life turned into what I think of as the world's most fucked-up geometry lesson. I'd developed, very quickly, two completely opposite lives that felt to me at the time like parallel lines: food and crack. And I plunged forward on those two tracks deeper and deeper in my pursuit of each of them every day.

If I hadn't dropped out of high school in ninth grade and had actually finished geometry class, I would've known better—in reality, both of the lines were at a steep 45-degree angle. One headed up, and the other down. It was only a matter of time before they intersected.

At Nora, my world was expanding exponentially, and I could tell that I was becoming a better chef every day, despite my drug use. Nora's focus on seasonal, organic food was still pretty revolutionary at that point, and it instilled in me an incredible respect for the product, which I still have today. Working there felt like taking a job at the original Garden of Eden—everything we used was fresh, perfect, and straight from the earth.

I'd been cooking for years, but my palate had suddenly exploded with possibilities. I tasted stinging nettles, pickled daikon, and kohlrabi for the first time. I was experimenting with different herbs and flours, spices and chilies. Every day, we made a different salad, and suddenly I had twelve or thir-teen different lettuces to choose from. I made soups with spring asparagus and mushroom oils, and paired fresh shrimp ceviches with mango, coconuts, and limes. I took the biggest, pinkest beets I had ever seen and served them seven different ways. And I learned how to cure a perfect fillet of salmon in salt and sugar under a brick until, a few days later, it turned into a gravlax that simply melted on your tongue.

The first morning that we had gotten stinging nettles in, Nora asked me to make a pasta with it, for service the next day. I'd made gnocchi and pierogi at Cha Bella, but we'd used dried pasta for everything else. At Nora, of course, everything had to be fresh. I'd never made pasta from scratch before, and didn't know how to do it.

Carlos was obviously an expert, churning out perfect batches before I'd even arrived at the restaurant. But I already felt like such an embarrassment around him that I didn't want to ask him. I whipped up a batch as best I could, and when I came in the next morning, it was in the trash, this big sticky mess hiding under a pile of carrot shavings. No one said anything, but I caught one of the Vietnamese prep cooks raising her eyebrows at me. She didn't have to tell me: It was shit.

Determined to figure it out on my own, I practiced for the next few nights until I found the secret, and was surprised at how simple it was—you just had to knead the hell out of the dough for a good five to seven minutes. It was a beautiful thing, making pasta from scratch. The pillowy pile of flour on the countertop, the eggs sitting in its deep well like a couple of birds in a nest, the simple, age-old ingredients coming together to form this universal food. It felt earthy, making pasta, almost pure.

Nora also ran an incredibly efficient kitchen, and I was picking up straight technique there, figuring out slowly how to pump out food. The littlest things made a huge difference in getting out three hundred plates a night. I'd always used tongs to handle meat, for example—at Nora, we used spoons. It was easier to be quick and still delicate with spoons, to flip the proteins without breaking them. I've not used tongs since.

Most kitchens I'd been in kept their sauces in little copper pots, but at Nora, they were in those plastic to-go coffee cups you'd take on a road trip. I'm talking everything—hollandaise, demi-glaces, you name it. It was ingenious. The cups were insulated, so the sauces stayed warm without keeping them on the heat. They were easy to handle, out of the way, and didn't break—perfect for the line.

I was starting to experiment more with my own technique, too. This was right around the first season of *Top Chef*, and everyone in the culinary world was going crazy over molecular gastronomy all of a sudden. It was the new movement in food and involved using science to harness pure flavors and deconstruct dishes. It was controversial and required the use of things like hydrocolloids and enzymes to achieve the unique textures and mediums it's known for, like foams and bubbles. Nora wasn't the place for that—if I'd pulled out xanthan gum in her kitchen, I might've gotten decked.

But there were moments. I made my first lobster bubbles there by accident, as a part of the crab dish I'd cooked during my stage. I was just whipping up some aioli and suddenly it felt like I'd captured the absolute essence of the lobster. Fucking amazing. Nora seemed to like it because it was done using egg yolks and not lecithin. Even though they are both natural products, if I could achieve the same effect without the use of what Nora called "chemicals," it seemed to be okay.

Things were going well, but overall it was a far from perfect situation. The actual cooking was going well, but I still stumbled every day with managing my staff. It was like bringing up a minor league ballplayer to the big leagues and immediately making him a coach. I barely knew what I was doing, but I was supposed to keep everyone else in line.

So I coped, essentially, by turning into an asshole. I might not have known much, but I clung to the things I did know, and then micromanaged the hell out them. I had to check every plate as it came off the line. I had to patrol the walk-in every night to make sure the product was stored properly.

I could tell the line cooks were getting antsy. They were fuckups like me, except Saint Carlos, but they mostly did a good job. And it was one thing to work with a fuckup, and completely another to be bossed around by one. Because I was their boss, I felt like I had to pull some kind of authority over them, and micromanaging was the only way I knew how. If I'd been on the line, I probably would've punched a guy like me.

One night, when I'd been there about a month, Nora's partner, Steven, pulled me off the line and into his office. He looked like fucking Santa Claus, big and burly with red cheeks and a thick, white beard. Nora had been with him for years—he'd been the manager of the Tabard Inn, where Nora had gotten her start in DC, and he and his brother had helped her open Restaurant Nora in the 1970s. They weren't married, but they'd lived together for as long as anyone could remember, and had two daughters.

Since Nora took care of the food side of everything—menu planning, products, special dishes—I hadn't seen much of Steven, who ran the rest of the operations. When he was at the restaurant, he stayed in his office, rarely coming into the kitchen at all. I was nervous about what he was going to say.

"So, Brandon," he said, motioning me to a chair across from him, "how have things been going?"

"Not too bad," I said, and for lack of anything better, launched into a review of that night's special. "I think the beet salad is really working well and then . . ."

"Listen, your food is fine," he said, cutting me off. "Nora's very happy with it. And when she's happy, I'm happy. But we're both wondering how everything else is going."

I hesitated. Were they talking about drugs? Did he know? Or just how things were going in the kitchen?

"We know you haven't managed a kitchen before. There's bound to be a learning curve."

I nodded. Was he going to fire me? Is this how it worked?

"And you know we want to use every resource we have to the best of our abilities. So if you think it's better to focus on your cooking, we can give some of the managerial responsibilities to Carlos."

The blood rushed back to my head in a wave of pure relief. Not only could I keep my job, but they were suggesting something that seemed, for the most part, ideal. I would get to do the part I really wanted to do, the part that I was really starting to nail down perfectly, without the part that was holding me back.

I was about to say yes, but something, some stubborn,

stupid lobe in my brain, told me not to. That taking this deal would be copping out, stunting my own growth as a chef in so many ways. That, eventually, I'd move on from Nora and I'd need to know how to do that as a manager as well as a cook. And that, if I said yes, they'd take a little part of my pride, too.

I respected Carlos, more than I'd ever respected anyone I'd worked with. And I knew in my gut that he deserved this opportunity more than I did. But the thought of his smug face taking over for me, even just partially, killed a little fire in my cocky, bravado-filled belly.

"I appreciate that, Steven. I really do," I said, choosing my words carefully. "But I think I can do this. I know I'm young and inexperienced. But I'm getting better every day. And I think I need to do this job—the whole job—to keep getting better."

I meant what I said. And if Nora had been the only thing in my life at that point, I know it would have been true. That this amazing culinary path I'd found was just winding out, and would have kept right on going to great places.

Unfortunately, the other path I was taking was moving just as quickly downward.

Skateboard and I had become like two peas in the world's most dysfunctional pod, meeting up every night after work without fail and smoking the night away. And I guess you could say we'd gotten close, or at least as close as you can get to a kid like him.

I didn't know much about his life, but he'd definitely been on the streets since he was thirteen or fourteen, completely on his own, stealing money at first to survive and then to feed his habit. When I met him, his main hustle was ATMs—he'd wait around when someone was getting cash, tooling around on his board so you didn't even notice him. Most people would leave after taking their money, forgetting to sign out of their account. The machine would ask if they wanted a new transaction, but they'd be long gone, and Skateboard would pounce.

Skateboard was as good at and as focused on smoking crack as Carlos was at cooking—and quickly he became just as much a mentor to me. He taught me where to find it, how to smoke it, when it was bad, and how to break it down. He knew everyone, and even though I'm not really sure why, other than the fact that I suddenly had a fair amount of cash every week, he let me know right away that he had my back. When we would see random beat downs or carjackings in the Northeast section of DC, he would make sure the people doing the deed knew I was with him and not some random fiend walking up and down the streets.

We started out smoking on the streets, like we'd done that first night. We'd duck into an alley, smoke a pipe, and then, with the drugs ripping through our bodies, we'd go back to the streets and start hollering at anyone we saw. Girls especially. Just vulgar, nasty shit. Things I'd never say in real life.

Skateboard lived on the border of Northeast, pretty much the most poverty-stricken and crime-filled neighborhood of the city, and after a few weeks, he told me that his roommates weren't home, so he could bring me back there to smoke instead of on the streets. I'm not sure what I expected, but Skateboard's room was just a dirty corner of floor in some fleabag apartment full of hipsters. He really didn't fit in at all with his roommates. I mean, the dude didn't even have any furniture. Just a pile in the corner, pairs of the same baggy jeans he wore every day.

We couldn't actually smoke in the apartment, so we ended up huddling by the window, smoking rocks and then dissolving into the same kind of shit we did on the street. That got old, too, and so one night when we were fresh out of rock, Skateboard said that, instead of going back to the street, it was time to meet Slim.

Slim also lived in Northeast, a little farther in from Skateboard, and as we got farther and farther in, I couldn't believe what I was seeing. I wasn't some coddled suburban kid—Jacksonville's pretty hood, and I thought I'd seen some fucked-up places in my day. But this was on a whole other level. Bombed-out buildings, busted old cars, pawnshops and liquor stores, addicts all over the streets. It was like hanging out in a real-life version of *Grand Theft Auto*.

Slim lived in a room in a boarded-up old house, and as we climbed the steps that first night, I could feel my stomach drop a little, knowing this wasn't a place I really wanted to be. Still, the promise of crack propelled me forward, motioning me to enter the foul-smelling room, to have a seat on the ratty, torn-up couch. There were box fans in every window, siphoning out the smoke, and nasty, yellowed sheets instead of blinds. A plywood board stood in for a table, propped up on milk crates, and Slim himself sat on a drumhead on the other side, like the lord of the crackheads.

Slim was well known in the DC crack scene, and that's literally how he introduced himself to me. "I'm Slim, you motha fucka. I'm a fucking legend."

Addicts flocked to him like wet on water. He was bald and emaciated, with cheeks sunken into pits under his eyes, and old as fuck. He looked to be at least fifty—just a pile of wrinkled skin and bones, sitting shirtless on his couch, smoking crack and holding court.

Slim was as fanatical about his crack as Nora was about her produce, and there was a ritual to his addiction. He'd get ahold of the rock and put it on a tray in front of him on the plywood board, where there was a Sterno can dripping down to an open fire. Most people recook their crack only if it's bad, but Slim cooked his every time, no matter if it was as pure as gold.

Right away he hooked up a deal for me, so I threw him a little bit of crack as a thank-you, which I could tell was the right thing to do, much as he made my skin crawl. He stood up from his drum as we were leaving that first night, and clasped his creepy, wrinkled claws on to my shoulders. His dirty nails were at least an inch long each, and dug into my shirt like a hypodermic needle.

"Remember dis. I'm Slim, you motha fucka," he repeated. "Nobody fuck wid you if you stay wid me."

So just like that, we had a standing invitation to come smoke at his house.

And that's the way life was for a couple of months—I'd cook at Nora's, go over to Slim's house with Skateboard and smoke the night away, and then take a cab back to Falls Church to sleep and do it all over again the next day.

About a month into all this, Chloe finally graduated and moved back up to Falls Church, and I thought it was the end. Up until that point, her parents had either turned a blind eye or really didn't know what the hell was going on, which actually was a distinct possibility. We had separate entrances, and even if I'd come straight home from work like a Boy Scout, they would've been asleep long before I got home, and at work by the time I left the next morning.

But the funny thing was, having her there didn't make one bit of difference. She knew I was using again—that was impossible to hide. And it's not as if she'd suddenly morphed into a saint, either. She still drank like a fish, and snorted lines with me every once in awhile. We still fought like banshees every night when I came home, lying about where I'd been. But she still didn't have any idea the depths of what I was getting into. When I was out with Skateboard, she thought I was drinking with Jessica or the line cooks. Maybe doing coke. Whatever. Enough to piss her off, but nowhere near the truth. She had begun to accept the fact that I was going to do what I want, but I think if she'd known I had started smoking crack, all bets would have been off.

And I was still holding my own at work, too, for the most part, by some miracle. There were still awkward moments with some of the kitchen staff, but I tried to use my conversation with Steven as a call to action with them. To be a better chef, I did have to be a better manager, and that meant gaining the trust of my staff one way or another. To them, I'm sure I was still a punk kid. But at least I didn't have to be a punk kid yelling at them about the Saran Wrap all night.

After that first, dismal day coming off crack, I'd learned how to control myself into getting my work done on the line, even when I was crashing. No matter how messed up I was, I just pushed through and cooked, and after that first morning, I never used at work again. The lows were still low—deeply, horribly so. I shudder even now just thinking back to some of those mornings, retching in the bathroom, my hands shaking with the daily withdrawal as I prepped.

But the only one who seemed to sense anything was going on at all was Carlos. I don't think he knew I was using drugs, per se, but he could definitely see that I was spending my time fucking off and not thinking about progressing the restaurant where he'd spent so much time. And let's be clear here: Cooks work hard, universally. But they also let loose in a major way. Alcohol and drug use isn't an exception in the kitchen, it's a rule. At Nora, too, even if the other cooks weren't smoking crack, I know they were still getting wasted every night. And I just happened to have this guy working below me with the stamina of a Navy SEAL and just as much self-discipline. Carlos was the anomaly, not me.

After a couple of months, though, I realized another thing about Carlos: He wasn't a snitch. He was better than me and he deserved my job, plain and simple. And we both knew it. But he was also proud as hell. He might've hated me with every fiber of his fucking body. Might've gone home every night after his glass of OJ and bitched to his wife about me until the sun came up. I know I would have, if I'd been in his shoes. But he was never going to complain to Nora.

So I'd reached this kind of status quo. Chloe and Carlos

were the only ones watching me, really, and while they both knew something was going on, neither was in any position to bust me. If Carlos said anything, he would look like a jealous, whiny sous chef and not the reserved and focused assistant that he was. He was better off waiting for me to self-sabotage my position. Chloe, on the other hand, just wanted to be with me and was happy to look the other way. The two lines of my life were still going to intersect: That was inevitable. But the surprising part was that I was still the one steering these courses. I had to be the one to make the paths cross.

When they did, it was amazingly unremarkable. I didn't screw up anything at work, didn't leave twenty pounds of lobsters on the counter or forget to show up for service or get high in the kitchen. I didn't steal from Chloe or her parents or crash their car or hit her or anything like that. There wasn't any event that made me realize I couldn't do it anymore. It may have been rock bottom, but it was a personal rock bottom, a private one.

I was out at Slim's house one night getting ready to smoke, as I had been every other night for the last two months, when I realized with sudden, total clarity that I didn't know anything about Slim or Skateboard. I'd spent more time with them than I had with my colleagues, my friends, even Chloe. And I didn't even know their real names.

During all the times I'd been over at Slim's, I'd seen other people only once or twice—hoppers delivering drugs. Other than that, it was always just the three of us. Slim didn't seem to have any friends or family. And other than those nights, I had no idea what these guys did with their lives. I knew they were stealing—there was no other way they'd have the money for the drugs. But what else? Had they raped people? Killed people? I wouldn't have been all that surprised. Most of our conversations were just about finding the next hit, and never got beyond that.

I felt a shiver climb up the back of my spine. I'd started doing drugs in kitchens in Savannah. But it was always with friends, coworkers, girlfriends, real people who I intersected with in real life. I'm not saying it was healthy, but it was a far cry from this dirty crack house I'd found myself in. I didn't know how I'd let myself get this far.

And just like I didn't know them, they didn't have any idea who I was, either.

They didn't know my name was Brandon. They just called me Chef. They didn't know that the night before, I'd made lamb with chickpeas and yogurt for a senator. They didn't know I came from Florida, that I was a drummer, that my girlfriend's name was Chloe, that I was the youngest chef de cuisine Nora had ever had. They couldn't have known any of that, because crack made me act like someone else.

Every morning when I'd wake up and come down off the drugs, that was what I regretted the most—that when I was high, I was not me. It's one thing to fuck up your body. I didn't care then about that. But I did care—deeply, even—about the fact that it was making me someone I didn't think I was. Crack is a street drug, through and through. And the streets have a way of making you harder, meaner. When I was on it, it was like the streets took over my personality, daring me to be the worst, grossest version of myself, fiending uncontrollably for sex and more drugs, contemplating stealing to get the next hit, things I would never dream of doing sober.

But until that moment, I didn't really grasp the reality of my descent.

Skateboard had never told me the details of his childhood, and I didn't have any idea what was going on with Slim. But I do know that outside of this sad drug world, this horribly depressing little family we'd built, they didn't seem to have anyone that gave a shit about them.

I resented my mom for a lot of things, but no matter how messed up she was, I know she always loved me. I had friends everywhere—in Jacksonville, Minneapolis, Savannah. I had a girlfriend who cared about me, and mentors at work who believed in me, even when I wasn't always sure they should have. And when I screwed up—and it was often—I had people who worried about me, who yelled at me, who begged me to do better. I might have hated them when they did. But for the first time, watching Slim and Skateboard, I realized how much worse it would have been if I didn't have these people in my life.

Sometimes even now, just sitting on my couch, I'll have a flashback to those nights, and it'll hit me like a punch in the stomach. They don't feel like normal memories. It's almost as if I've repressed something terrible from my childhood, and someone's just told me that it happened, and I have to go back and remember it as if it was the first time. And I'll be right back in it, getting high and fucking some faceless girl as if she was nothing.

I've thought of Slim and Skateboard both plenty of times in the six years since I left DC—Skateboard especially. He's not someone you can just look up on Facebook or whatever. But I wonder about him. If, by some miracle, he ever got clean. Or, in the far more likely scenario, if he died.

I know that if I'd stayed in DC, I would've been well on my way down that path, too. And I knew it that night, waiting for my turn on the pipe, as clearly as if I'd been to a psychic. For the first time in the last two months, there was a need in my head even more urgent than my need to smoke: I had to get out of there. Before I could change my mind, I picked up my shit, kicked back the plywood table, and left, running out of the hood, and hailing a cab back to Virginia as soon as I saw one.

Addiction still had a hold on me, and I wasn't quite ready to go back to rehab or go totally cold turkey. But I knew I had to get things under control. If using in DC meant crack, that meant I had to get out of DC. Even if it meant giving up Nora.

I stayed up that whole night, sitting in the window of our bedroom at Chloe's parents' condo, smoking cigarettes and trying to formulate a plan. And when the sun rose, my head felt clearer than it had in weeks. I showered, brushed my teeth, wandered outside to get the paper, and when Chloe woke up, I was sitting at the kitchen table circling any ads for chef jobs outside of the city.

But there was still one thing I had to do.

I couldn't bring myself to go in to work and face Nora. She had believed in me, had given me a chance when, probably, no one had deserved it less. I'd always loved cooking, but Nora showed me a world of food I'd never even dreamed about. And not only that, she had put that world in the palm of my hand and told me to run with it. I'd squandered it instead, and the guilt I felt over that fact had crippled me—had kept me in the condo kitchen when I should have gotten on the Metro and gone in to talk to Nora myself.

Instead, I sent her a text. I was resigning, effective immediately, and leaving the city as soon as possible. There was nothing she could say that would change my mind, no matter how hard she tried.

It was one of the first times I remember really giving up on a dream. It wouldn't be the last.

CHAPTER TWO

Chestertown, Maryland, on the banks of the Chester River, is probably exactly what you're picturing. A small town with nothing but a 7-Eleven, a grocery store, a flower shop, and a rickety wooden fish shack. There were old, colonial brick houses, more marinas than parking lots, and a parade every Memorial Day when people dressed up like Revolutionary War soldiers. In other words, after spending six months in DC crack houses, it was exactly what I needed.

I'd found an ad on the Internet, when I was still in DC, for a sous chef job at the Imperial Hotel in Chestertown and jumped on it, even though it was a step down from what I'd been doing on all fronts. The Imperial doesn't have a bad reputation, especially in the Mid-Atlantic, but it's no Nora. And this time I knew for sure that I wasn't interviewing for the chef de cuisine job. But I didn't care. I needed to chill out and get my head on straight while I figured out my next move.

And maybe, after Nora, there were worse things than a piece of humble pie.

Chloe hadn't found a job yet in DC, so she was down to make the move, too. Together, we packed up her car and left her parents' condo in Falls Church, getting the hell out of there as fast as we could. Looking into the side mirror of the U-Haul, I saw her parents smiling and waving all proud-like, as if they felt we were finally doing something on our own, without their help or financial assistance. As we left the city limits behind us, crawling up 95 past Baltimore and over the Bay Bridge to the Eastern Shore, I could already feel myself breathing easier. I rolled down the windows and let the salty bay breeze wash over me, dreaming of eating steamed crabs with Chloe, cracking them open on big, newspaper-covered tables, hands gritty with Old Bay.

I wasn't sure what to expect when we rolled up to the Imperial Hotel, but the name kind of says it all. It's a little boutique operation—only twelve rooms total, and they're all in a giant plantation-style house with white columns and a wide wraparound porch. There's not a whole lot to do there except sit on the porch and look at the river, but I guess that's enough for some people.

The hotel was built more than one hundred years ago, but when I showed up, it had just been sold, which made the situation different from what I'd anticipated, reading the ad back in DC. The new owner was this military guy who'd just retired and who bought the hotel on the condition that his son, a twenty-eight-year-old chef, could run the restaurant.

That chef turned out to be Tom Pizzica, future runner-up

on *The Next Food Network Star* and now the host of the Food Network's *Outrageous Food*. He's pretty famous now, but at that point, he wasn't so different from me—a talented chef but kind of a fuckup, with a girlfriend in tow, some experience working with big-name chefs (but hacks like Wolfgang Puck big, not Thomas Keller big), no experience running his own larger-scale fine dining restaurant, and more than an occasional fondness for ending his shift with a noseful of coke. If you've seen any of Tom's shows, you have some idea of what he looks like—big, curly-haired, with a shit-eating grin on his face most of the time—and when he came out to the front porch to meet me that first day, I knew we'd get along fine.

Tom had reopened the old restaurant at the Imperial as The Front Room and was focusing on classics, with a nod toward Maryland seafood, of course. I knew he'd been working in California, under Wolfgang Puck for a while, and I was excited to see what kind of food he was putting out.

It happened that most of the menu was basic comfort food, especially at lunch. Meat loaf and mashed potatoes. Mac and cheese. Fish-and-chips. Pork chops. Kind of a snooze. But he did have a few cool tricks up his sleeve that made me think of some of the classic dishes in a different way. He glazed his monkfish with tamarind paste and served his grouper with risotto made with juiced asparagus and milk. I was amused, much later, to see that one of his most successful dishes on *The Next Food Network Star* was pork tenderloin with mustard spaetzle, which he developed at the Imperial. I was glad he was still using it, and not entirely surprised that he got so far with it. It's a good, simple dish, especially the spaetzle, which I still occasionally use on menus to this day, too.

And then there were Tom's crab cakes. It's dangerous business to fuck with crab cakes on the Eastern Shore of Maryland. It's like rethinking clam chowder in Boston or lobster rolls in Maine or fish tacos in San Diego. Locals know better, and guests are coming for the real thing. But Tom somehow beat the system—by using scallop mousse as his only binder, the crab cakes were rich and a little more sophisticated, but still maintained an authentic Maryland crab flavor. He served them with a roasted Granny Smith apple puree and brussels, and I gotta say, it was a nice plate of food. I didn't really have much of a say in any of the dishes, but I also didn't mind the food that Tom was putting out. And as long as I was learning something new, I stayed content.

From my perspective, Tom couldn't actually manage a restaurant for shit, and even though he was seven years older than me, we had pretty much the same amount of experience. He wasn't much of a boss, but he did become a friend, and after a while, we managed to drum up a bit of a good time, even in sleepy Chestertown. Tom was a city guy, too, who hadn't been in Chestertown for much longer than I had—he'd grown up near Philly but had been in San Francisco for the last five years and wasn't quite sure how to handle small-town life, either.

What neither Tom nor I knew at that point was that Chestertown had a dark side, thanks to its location just about an hour east of Baltimore, which is just as fucked up as *The Wire* makes it seem. When people got in trouble in

Baltimore, they'd often come up to Chestertown to wait it out for a while. That meant a deceptively high proportion of shady motherfuckers hanging around. And this also meant plenty of drugs, even though I'd come to Chestertown to get away from them.

One of the shadiest characters around happened also to be one of the prep cooks, a Dominican dude from Baltimore named James, who used to try to sell us heroin in little orange gelcaps. Heroin scared me. The dope fiends I'd seen always seemed to be in a perpetual state of zombielike behavior. I know that sounds arbitrary when I'd just spent several months with my mouth glued to a crack pipe, but there is a sort of hierarchy to using, and I'd never done heroin before. Coke is one level, crack is another, and heroin and meth seemed like hitting the fucking rooftop. It might have just been that heroin wasn't as accessible in places I'd been, but either way, it scared the fuck out of me. And James was one hard-ass dude, on a level that I'd rarely seen before. He used to tell stories about gang shit going down in Baltimore, and I didn't want any part of it. I'd literally cover my ears, tell him I didn't want to know, and walk away.

But that dude could push. One night, when Tom and I were drinking in the kitchen after a shift, James showed up again with the little orange gelcaps and kept pestering me, like the world's scariest insect, and I felt I couldn't say no again. I opened the capsule, which was full of this brownish powder, and snorted it quickly, bracing myself for the worst (or, maybe even worse than the worst, bracing myself to love it). But I swear to God, I felt nothing. It's true that I was off-my-ass drunk that night, but as fucked up as I was, there was no way I wouldn't have felt that much straight heroin. I was playing Russian roulette, almost as if I'd had a gun pointed to my head and I'd spun a blank. I was pissed as all get-out since I'd just gotten screwed out of some money for what clearly wasn't anything, but also because part of me wanted to know what was so great about the drug. The fact that it was fake was, of course, lucky as hell for me. Heroin was a road that I couldn't be led down.

After this, I started to figure out James's hustle. He'd push his "heroin" to us assholes in Chestertown all week and then go back to Baltimore on the weekends and buy real shit with the money. He'd be high the whole weekend and show up at work on Monday dope sick and ready to start the cycle again. Another kitchen success story.

The dishwashers at the Imperial were both good guys, in a Tweedledee-Tweedledum kind of way. Frank was white and fit, with a thick, sandy-colored mustache and a shaved head. He was way too smart to be washing anyone's dishes, and actually seemed interested in food, which still makes me wonder why he wasn't cooking. Jarrell was big and slow and would've been a dead ringer for Bubba from *Forrest Gump*, if only Bubba had a side hustle of delivering cocaine to me and the cooks between shifts.

But my favorite character in Chestertown, hands down, was Paul, the Imperial Hotel's bartender. I swear to God, this dude seemed like he was in the witness protection program. I always thought in the back of my mind that he had to be a shot caller for some Northeastern branch of the mob. He was creepy and gaunt and wore suits and mafioso hats and shook a cocktail like he was Frank Sinatra's wingman. But, to make matters even weirder, he lived in a little wooden shack by the river, like a total redneck. The only electricity I ever saw him use was to play his phonograph, which would spin vinyls pressed with melodies from the 1920s. He'd take me fishing for striped bass—or what Marylanders called rockfish—and then we'd sit together on his porch, drinking scotch and talking about books. He's one of the strangest dudes I've ever met, and I loved him.

I'd been traveling around from city to city for years at that point—since I was a teenager—but at heart, I'm a bayou boy, with salt water running through my veins right along next to my blood. When I was out fishing with Paul, in a boat on the open water, crickets chirping and humid air radiating around me, I'd think about home, and especially about my family.

I grew up mostly in Jacksonville, Florida, but I was born in Morgan City, Louisiana, which is a little shrimping town on the banks of the Atchafalaya River, and that's where my roots are, right down to my last name, which I got from my grandmother, although my mother didn't use it. She was a huge part of my childhood and taught me to love the open water as much as she did.

My grandmother was a Morgan City native, too, born Andrea Gustava Jenkins in 1939 to two childhood neighbors from Thunderbolt, Georgia—Miriam Price and Charles Moses ("C.M.") Jenkins. He traveled a lot for work, mostly where the shrimp swam, in the Gulf of Mexico. They jumped from port to port in Louisiana, Texas, and Mississippi, settling only for a few months at a time, which wasn't an easy way for my grandmother to grow up. After moving constantly and eating only what she called "fruits of the gulf," she contracted a life-threatening bacterial infection that persisted throughout five years of her childhood.

Things got harder when her father, C.M., gave up his shrimping career to become a tugboat captain. It seemed like a more stable life for a time, until his tugboat capsized in a "rogue wave" in the Devil's Triangle, just off the coast of Florida, where my mother would later be born. The sole witness said he saw my great-grandfather's legs hit his face in the water, and he knew they were broken and there was no hope.

My grandmother was married four times before I was born—my mother, Amber, was from the second husband—and twice afterward, but it was her fifth husband, John Baltzley, who left an indelible mark on my grandmother, my mother, and me. He left us his name, in the most complicated, fucked-up way possible.

To explain how my grandmother came to marry John Baltzley, and how I, with not a drop of German blood in my veins, came into a German surname, it's important to understand how I was born. Most children are conceived in an act of love, even if it goes to shit before they're born. For me, it was a little different.

My mother grew up a navy brat, spending her childhood on bases in Hawaii and Jacksonville. By the time she was twenty-one, my mother was living back in Morgan City, where she was helping my grandmother, who was down with a bad back. My mother is a lesbian, and she was dating a woman named Susan Baltzley. Throughout the course of their relationship, their families got to know one another, and my grandmother started spending time with Susan's father, who was also single. They got married when I was four, and my grandmother took John's last name.

My mother spent most of her time with Susan and with her best friend, Tally, who had an acquaintance named Jim Marque, a Cajun who grew dope out in the swamps nearby. One night, Jim showed up at my mother's house drunk as hell. She didn't want him to come in, but she let him because she was afraid he was going to kill someone on his way back to his house in Bayou Corn. But he ended up forcing himself on her, and pretty soon after that, she found out she was pregnant.

The decision to have me wasn't easy on my mother, especially because she didn't have any health insurance. But she couldn't quite bring herself to have an abortion, so she made the gut-wrenching decision to marry Susan Baltzley's brother to get the insurance. It was purely a business transaction—she met her "husband" only a few times. He was stationed in Germany in the army and was living with a German woman— getting married got him off the hook for that, so it was convenient for both of them. She took Baltzley as her last name and gave it to me, too, and later, when my grandmother married John, she took it as well. Even though neither marriage lasted—my mother's or her mother's—all three of us have kept the Baltzley name to this day, and will until we die. It may not have started as our family name, but it is now.

With a new baby in hand, my mother realized that she couldn't keep dicking around in Morgan City, so she packed me up and moved to Florida, in large part to be near her mother, who had moved with John into a condo in Green Cove Springs, about twenty miles west of Jacksonville and directly on the St. Johns River. During the day, my grandmother (or Branny Annie, as I called her) was a legal clerk. But what she really lived for was fishing. I don't think there was a single dry day that she wasn't out on the water.

When I went out fishing with Paul in Chestertown that first time, I couldn't help but smile, thinking of Branny Annie and how much she would've loved it up there. Maybe even with Paul, who seemed like he would've been perfect for her in another life. Her husband, John, liked fishing, too, but it seemed to be the only thing they had in common. They couldn't even agree on football—she was a Florida Gators fan, and he rooted for the Florida State Seminoles. But when they were out on their boat, *Tailfeather*, things were always at peace.

Sitting in Paul's boat, I'd think about afternoons in Green Cove Springs—speeding up the river, skipping waves, the smells of gasoline, suntan lotion, and fish in the sun. A lot of times we would take the boat all the way into downtown Jacksonville to The Landing, where we would dock and go to Hooters, Fat Tuesdays, or Lubi's. I'd get food, and the adults would start in on beers and margaritas, and that's how we'd pass the afternoons. My favorite, though, was sitting still on the water and watching my grandma and mom fish. I'd crack open Cokes and cans of Vienna sausages while

I waited for something to happen. Every now and then, the excitement would pick up when someone would accidentally catch a stingray or eel. That's when Branny would pounce. She'd pick up her stick and proceed to beat the living shit out of them on the side of the boat, cussing and yelling at my mom to not let them in the boat. If anyone wondered where my take-no-shit attitude comes from, I'd direct them to an old lady in a fishing boat right outside Jacksonville.

∽

I'd been in Chestertown a few months, chilling out, cooking, drinking, and doing a bunch of coke, when I started to get a little restless. The menu at the Imperial Hotel was decent, but I was also starting to feel myself slipping backward. One of the most eye-opening parts about working at Nora was the product—she went out of her way to get everything local and organic, from Amish farms, and I missed this approach to cooking. It was just impossible in Chestertown, which wasn't on a standard route for good farms or purveyors, so the product suffered immensely. Instead of milk-fed veal, we were stuck with oxidized beef flown in from Texas from companies like Sysco or U.S. Foodservice. Out-of-season crab came in cans, and chicken was frozen in cases of twenty-four. Without that fresh, flavorful produce and meat, I didn't feel I was honing my technique or doing the kind of cooking that I really wanted to be doing.

Plus, I was ready for some new menu challenges. I love comfort food—my favorite meal is and always will be a greasy brown-paper sack of fried chicken from Union Pig and Chicken in Pittsburgh—but I was also ready to stretch my limits a little, see what else was out there. And pretty soon I had my chance.

One night, a few months in, I had the opportunity to cook a tasting menu for Brigit Binns, a cookbook author from California with major connections in the New York food scene. We didn't get a lot of those types in Chestertown, so we took her visit seriously.

There wasn't anything particularly groundbreaking about the menu I cooked for Brigit. I added only one of my own dishes—a risotto with crab, green apple, cider vinegar, and saffron. But I took care to cook everything else perfectly. My meats were pulled, seasoned, seared, basted, rested, and cut properly. Vegetables were cooked through and seasoned with salt, vinegar, herbs, and butter, not overwhelmed with a strong spice like pepper. It was all basic technique--things most chefs should learn in their first year of culinary school and that I'd perfected at Nora, but things that made an enormous difference, especially with that kind of simple food.

I took my time with the risotto, elongating the cooking time to coax it gently and gradually into releasing its starches. Instead of chicken stock, I added a fumet I had made from the striped bass carcass and some shellfish we had lying around. The extra time that I took allowed the swamp grass seed to spread on the bowl while still holding its circular composition, ensuring that every grain was perfectly cooked and held the integrity of its shape. I always think of the shape of the grain when plating my risotto. I've made risottos from oats, rice, potatoes, and apples by cutting the potatoes and apples in a small dice and treating them like grains. When they're done, every grain should firmly maintain its shape while staying loose and integrating into the dish. It may sound pretentious as hell, but risotto is important and I take it very seriously.

After the meal, Brigit called me into the dining room to chat. I could tell right away that she was a giant flirt, and usually, that tends to work in my favor. As we talked, she started telling me about people she worked with and knew in New York. And it turned out that one of her closest friends was Doug Psaltis's brother.

I knew about Doug Psaltis, of course. He'd worked under everyone from David Bouley to Alain Ducasse to Thomas Keller. And now he was back in New York, opening an enormous new restaurant in the Carlton Hotel on Park Avenue with Geoffrey Zakarian, called Country. This was the opposite of meat loaf and fish-and-chips—it had a grand formal dining room upstairs and a more casual menu downstairs, though even the downstairs room wasn't really slumming it, with menu items like a foie appetizer. The tasting menu upstairs seemed to be pushing limits of excess—foie terrines, sea urchin, duck tartes, everything coming with a rich velouté. It wasn't just New York dining—it was New York dining made to feel like Europe.

I wasn't sure I would always want to do food like that, but I did know that if I was going to take my culinary career seriously, I needed fine dining experience, and that wasn't going to happen in Chestertown. So, when Brigit crooked her finger at me, motioning me to lean in close as she asked sweetly, "What the hell are you doing in this dipshit town when I can get you a stage at Country tomorrow?" I had to admit that I didn't have a good answer for her. And so I told her, "Make the call."

CHAPTER THREE

It's easy to think you know it when you actually have no fucking idea. Because New York isn't just one city, it's a million, all rolled up into one. And, as I was soon to find out, one man's New York could have absolutely nothing to do with another's.

I'd been to New York about five times previously, all while I was touring with Kylesa as a teenager. We played everything from Brooklyn house shows to sold-out venues in Manhattan, such as The Bowery Ballroom.

But when I rolled up to Park Avenue South to start my stage at Country, it was like I'd never been in this city at all. I guess it goes without saying that, when you're touring with a metal band, you don't usually end up on Park Avenue, and Doug Psaltis's Country was Park Avenue to the max.

Country, and its downstairs "café," were in the lobby of the Carlton Hotel, a cavernous space that Zakarian had just pumped millions into renovating. There was a giant glass bar in the middle of the restaurant, and chandeliers dripping with crystals everywhere. The kitchen was coated in copper and steel and was immaculately clean. I'd heard that Country was supposed to be the "rustic" counterpart to Zakarian's other restaurant, Town, but that was a joke. This was the fanciest, stuffiest, most un-rustic restaurant I'd ever been in, right down to the kitchen. Because it was an open kitchen on display to every power luncher, rich-ass tourist, and douche-bag banker in the dining room, the renovations in the kitchen had been just as important as anywhere else in the restaurant. And fuck, was it beautiful. Probably the most beautiful kitchen I've ever worked in even to this day, and at that point in my career, it completely blew me away.

On Brigit's recommendation, I'd been invited to come up for a two-day stage, which is something I never would have gotten if it hadn't been for her. And not only that, but her word had gotten me a good station, too. I showed up in the kitchen fully expecting to be put on garde manger, which is the cold station where salads and canapés are made— definitely the lowest place on the totem pole. But instead, Psaltis greeted me, knew exactly who I was, and sent me directly over to fish, where I'd be working with another cook, a young black-Irish guy who had a wide-eyed, sort of shell-shocked look to him.

Doug Psaltis seemed like a nice guy when I first met him, but I could tell as soon as we got into the kitchen that, in fact, he was a giant motherfucker. He was constantly in someone's face, berating them for every tiny little mistake, and even some things that didn't seem to be mistakes at all. He was a charmer with customers, but when he got in front of his employees, it was like he turned into some kind of demonic lord who wanted his subjects to cower in fear at his feet. Nora, on the other hand, was the opposite. Nora could be stubborn and at times that would make it hard to work with her, but she definitely cultivated a friendly atmosphere whereas Psaltis was pretty much a fearmonger.

For the most part, it worked. The cooks that I met staging were scared shitless, watching Psaltis bitch out their colleagues, knowing that it would be them, too, soon enough. Toward the end of the second day, he called out one of the female cooks who was working the hot apps line. Oddly enough, her name was Brandon, too, and I could feel my stomach drop as the two syllables bounced off the kitchen walls. I can't remember what she'd done wrong—something pretty minor, I think— but Psaltis dragged her to the front of the pass anyway. There was a chef's table in the Country kitchen, and a twelve-person party was seated there for a tasting menu. Psaltis stood her in front of the diners and lit into her, screaming and cussing and finally, in front of everyone, calling her a lazy cunt. Needless to say, it was awkward for all involved.

I must've done something right, because at the end of the stage, Psaltis offered me the job. And I'll never forget the look on his face when I turned his ass down. It was a cocky move on my part—we both knew I'd gotten the stage by the skin of my teeth and that I needed this opportunity to break into the

New York culinary scene. But as much as Country had to offer—a good reputation, a high-end product, and the fucking kitchen of my dreams—I just couldn't imagine putting up with that bullshit every day. So I left Psaltis looking thoroughly confused and put off, but I knew, despite the irksome feeling of turning down a solid job, that I had made the right decision.

Country might not have been the right fit for me, but as soon as I left after my second night there, I knew I wouldn't be going back to the Imperial Hotel, either. Chestertown was a cool place to hang out and flip crab cakes for a few months, but I knew that if I was ever going to get serious about my career, it had to be in New York. Plus, I figured, if I could please that asshole, someone else was bound to hire me somewhere. I had come up for a two-day stage, but I wouldn't leave for another five years.

My mom told me over and over again when I was growing up that I should always have a fallback job, in case the one I had didn't work out. A dream job is a dream job, she said, but you always have to make sure you can pay your bills. She was talking about my music career then, but cooking sometimes doesn't feel all that different from drumming. It was advice that stuck with me, and would become particularly important when I moved to New York.

As a kid, school was always kind of a mixed bag. I knew I was smart—I did well on all the bullshit standardized tests they gave us, and when I was good at something or if something held my interest, I always got straight As. But, just as I would jump from job to job later in life, I got bored easily. Things were either too easy for me or they didn't interest me, and I didn't see much use in paying attention when I wasn't interested. No one in my family had much education, and while my mom wanted me to do well, it was just as important to her that I learned to make my own way in the world, through education or not.

When I was going into ninth grade, I had an opportunity that could have really changed things for me educationally—I was accepted into the International Baccalaureate program at the Paxon School for Advanced Studies, across town from the high school I was supposed to attend in Jacksonville. Instead of going to the shitty local schools that I'd been in since I was a kid, I was going to be in a competitive magnet program that would prepare me for college and beyond. But I wasn't into it. The only thing I cared about at that point was music. I'd been playing in bands with my neighborhood friends for years, and we still got together on weekends and after school, but that's where I wanted to be all the time. I tried to get along with the kids at my new school—I played the third bass drum in the drum line and I even joined the step team. Yes, the championship motherfucking step team. Complete with cornrows and a big blue-and-white-striped cane. But even that didn't work. I started getting into fights all the time and slipping in my classes, and about halfway through my freshman year, I was kicked out of the program.

I transferred to my neighborhood school, Lee High School, halfway through my freshman year, but I'd already missed so much that the principal told me I'd have to repeat ninth grade. I was old for my grade anyway, and it was getting embarrassing to be held back. I had other things going on—I was playing music in a couple of different bands, and I'd just gotten my first full-time job, at the Cool Moose Café. It was supposed to be a dishwashing gig, something to put a little cash in my pocket. But within a week, I was cooking on the line. And I fucking loved it. I had finally found something that held my attention not just through first period, but through every single grueling hour of my shift. Knowing that I was going to have to repeat a year, I basically stopped going to class. Most days, I'd walk to school, go to band practice, and then leave. I'd go hang out by the river, smoke cigarettes, watch boats, and dodge cops. Then I'd go home or go to work.

On January 23, 2002, I turned seventeen and was still in the ninth grade, so my mom gave me a choice: I could stay in school and make a better effort not to get expelled. Or I could quit. But there was a caveat. If I dropped out, I had to start working full-time and contributing to the bills. I'd have to learn to have a backup plan—she wasn't going to bail me out if things didn't work out at the Cool Moose, or wherever I was working. The choice was clear. I upped my hours at the restaurant and dropped out of school, and haven't stepped in a classroom since. Though it's not the traditional road to success, I can't imagine any other path working for me.

But I have gotten very skilled at the art of the fallback. I was right about one thing when I quit the Imperial Hotel—there were jobs to be had in New York kitchens, and Doug Psaltis wasn't the only asshole willing to give them to me, even if I was woefully unprepared. My first year in New York was about to become a blurry montage of them—chef after chef, some kind and talented and generous, some cocky and insecure and downright hostile. There were big, beautiful kitchens like Country, and tiny closets with a few burners and a convection oven. There were restaurants that would earn raves from *The New York Times* and ones that would close within weeks. My resume grew longer and longer, each entry like a little tile in a patchy mosaic on the walls of a subway station—sometimes surprisingly beautiful, sometimes ugly and worn and covered in piss.

It started at Giorgione 508, the newish Northern Italian restaurant from Giorgio DeLuca of Dean & DeLuca fame, where, within a week of moving up to New York, I had an interview as a sous chef. At that point, my only experience with Italian cooking was from Cha Bella in Savannah, which basically meant jack shit but gave me enough bravado to act, I'm sure, like an asshole. I could make a wild mushroom ravioli and a deconstructed pesto flatbread that I thought, however misguided it might have been, was genius. It was all jacked up and wrong, but I didn't care. How hard could it possibly be to learn the rest?

There was a new chef at 508—Massimiliano Bartoli, or Chef Max, as we called him, and he looked like something straight out of a Michelangelo painting. He was always dressed head to toe in white, like an angel with a chef's knife—white clogs, white chef's pants, and a pristine, two-hundred-dollar, white chef's coat—and the ensemble was topped off with thousand-dollar Versace eyeglasses. You could practically hear harps playing when he walked into the room. Chef Max could obviously tell right away that I didn't have serious experience with Italian cuisine, but he could see promise in me, and decided to give me a chance as sous chef.

For a fleeting minute, it seemed like everything was working out as best as it possibly could. Just months after the plummet in DC, I'd picked myself back up and scored a job in a legit New York City kitchen. And with that came a major attitude change. I'm not sure if it was what I'd seen, both from Psaltis during my Country stage and also on shows like Gordon Ramsay's *Hell's Kitchen*, which was just starting to become famous, but I had this idea that, in order to run a kitchen, I had to be a complete and total dick. I'm sure some of it came from my insecurity at Nora, too. I'd been jealous of Carlos's discipline, and, when I started out at 508, I wanted to give off the air that I had that kind of discipline, too.

Immediately, I set up a regimen of rules. Music was 86'd from the kitchen. We were there to cook, I reasoned, not to have a fucking dance party. Remembering the trick that I learned at Nora, I banned all tongs from the kitchen in favor of spoons. If I saw a single pair lying around, I threw it away, even if it personally belonged to one of the cooks. Even talking was strictly prohibited. I wasn't going to tolerate mistakes, I told myself, and I made sure my staff knew it.

The problem, of course, is that I didn't know what the fuck I was talking about. Sure, I knew how to cook some things. But I didn't yet have the subtle touch I'd need to really master Italian cooking.

About a month into my tenure there, Giorgio himself

came into the kitchen to see how I was fitting in, and asked me to make him a plate of spaghetti pomodoro. Like the simple omelet in classical French cooking, pomodoro is the ultimate test of an Italian cook's chops. When done right, it can be exquisite. When it's wrong, you might as well go to the fucking Olive Garden. I did the best I could, but I left the aromatics—basil and garlic—in the sauce when I served it to him. A rookie mistake. Giorgio took one bite, and then looked at Chef Max and shook his head. I wasn't supposed to hear him, but I did.

"I just don't think Brandon gets it." I didn't lose my job right then, but I did lose my motivation. Hearing that was enough to make me shed the pretense of discipline and stop what I actually had been doing for the first few weeks on the job—learning how to cook like an Italian. A few weeks later, I went out after a shift with the bartender and his fiancée and ended up on the roof of their Williamsburg loft with an eight ball of coke. It doesn't even matter what happened that night—it was like a thousand before it and like a thousand would be after it. But what did matter was that I knew I wouldn't be returning to Giorgione after that, except to pick up my knives.

My failure at Giorgione was a hefty blow to what had become a pretty inflated ego, and after that, I fell into a long series of unmemorable gigs at restaurants around the city that did little except add to my reputation, which was growing in both good and bad ways. I was junior sous chef at Michael Psilakis's Anthos, sous chef at Pichet Ong's P*ong, chef de partie at Little Giant, chef de partie at Susur Lee's Shang, chef de partie at Wallse . . . and on and on and on the list went. I was rarely anywhere for more than a month, sometimes even less. Sure, I was learning things—picking up technique and flavor profiles and ideas for dishes here and there, cobbling together my own low-rent version of culinary training. But after a while, I'd screw something up, or piss off the chef, or stay out all night fucking around and miss a shift. Nothing was really speaking to me, and at that point, I honestly couldn't give much of a shit.

A huge reason for my lack of focus in the kitchen was, of course, what was going on outside of it, which is a common theme in kitchens all across the country and, I imagine, the world. I've heard many theories attempting to explain the abundance of drugs and alcohol in kitchens. A kitchen is a high-paced, competitive, and sometimes stressful place, so maybe having a common vice tying everyone together is somehow a comfort. It could just as easily be that the type of person who wants to spend time in the hectic yet repetitive environment of a kitchen probably has a somewhat addictive personality. Sometimes I don't know how anyone gets fed at all, given that they're being fed by a bunch of drunk, high assholes every night.

But for me, it hadn't always been that way. As I spent my first year leaping from job to job in New York, I started to wonder how I'd gotten to this point. Sure, I'd never exactly been a goody-goody, and I stole my fair share of my mom's beer and cigarettes when I was a kid. But given that I'd basically been on my own since I was a teenager, and that I floated between the food world and the metal world, both infamous for their rampant substance abuse, sometimes I'm actually amazed that it took me until I was eighteen to really get into drugs.

It took me until Savannah.

I ended up in Savannah on kind of a whim. And as with many moves that would come later in my life, this one was because of a girl, or at least it was in the beginning. I was eighteen years old when I first met Lisa and was still living in Jacksonville, sharing an apartment with my childhood friend Scott and another cook named Josh and playing in a band called Striking at Hawthorne. It was a fun time—we lived behind a gay bar called the Metro, which housed five different bars within it, and we spent most of our time hanging out there or going to shows—but I had lived in Jacksonville my whole life, and I was definitely getting restless.

Lisa and I had connected through MySpace, and she offered to drive down to Jacksonville one weekend to meet me. I had no idea what to expect. All I knew was that she was older—twenty-six to my eighteen—and liked my kind of music. But when she emerged from her Land Rover, I was pleasantly surprised. She was all of five feet four, and a hundred pounds soaking wet, which made for quite a sight standing next to the Land Rover, but she was fucking cute as hell. And I knew immediately that she was down for a good time.

We had a wild night—this girl could drink like no one I had ever seen before, and she knew her music, which was a winning combination in my book. We started out the night at a downtown club called The Imperial, where she put away more tequila than any girl her size should be able to drink, then drove around Jacksonville listening to music, and finally ended up at my place, where we had the most intense sex I'd ever had. She grabbed my hair and forced me onto the bed so hard that the bed fell over and broke the door. It was fierce, and I'd never been so attracted to anything in my life. She left the next day, heading back north for an afternoon class at the Savannah College of Art and Design, but invited me to come up the next weekend for a visit.

I couldn't wait to see Lisa again, and I was also intrigued by Savannah itself. I'd just seen the movie *Midnight in the Garden of Good and Evil*, and fell in love with the creepy veils of Spanish moss, and the old graveyards. It's not far from Jacksonville, and though my friends and I had never been, we'd heard tons of stories—weird people and unbelievable beauty.

Savannah was one of the only cities in the South left unburned after the Civil War—it was spared because it was so beautiful, even the North couldn't bear to see it ruined. Streets were shaded from the sun by overgrown trees that met with a kiss from each side and drooled down Spanish moss that you could almost touch if you held your arms to the sky. There were no buildings more than four stories high, and rows and rows of gorgeous, colorful old houses. Lisa's was no different, and when I pulled up in front of her gigantic, two-hundred-year-old mustard-colored house and saw her smoking her American Spirit Light on the front porch out of a pack that matched the color of her house, something told me I'd be staying for a while.

The plan, of course, was just to stay for the weekend. But if

I'd been hooked on the drive in, then the weekend only cemented things. We spent the entire day at Bonaventure Cemetery, way out in Thunderbolt, Georgia, where my great-grandmother and great-grandfather had been born and raised. I was looking for the iconic statue Bird Girl from the cover of *Midnight in the Garden of Good and Evil*, but it had been moved to the Telfair Museum downtown. Still, there was plenty of creepy shit around—decrepit stuffed teddy bears on children's graves, and a vast network of tombs along the banks of the Savannah River. If they're still accepting any bodies when the last of my nine lives run out, I can't think of anywhere I'd rather be buried.

I was underage when I first visited Savannah—only eighteen—but that didn't seem to matter. Savannah was one hell of a drinking town. I've lived in a lot of drinking towns, but Savannah is definitely at the top. The first night, we went to a big, two-story wine bar that would soon become a staple in my life. It was dark and mellow and I didn't have a problem getting served, but there was also a weird vibe that I couldn't quite put my finger on.

That first weekend flew by, and on the third day, it was time to say good-bye and head home. But Lisa and I couldn't quite do it, and when she asked me on a total whim if I'd consider moving in with her, I didn't hesitate. Lisa was worldly, beautiful, artistic, and, best of all, not in Jacksonville. I'd never lived anywhere else, except for a few disastrous months in Louisiana when I was twelve, and I was itching for something new. I had no friends in Savannah, no job, and no prospects. But I also knew that I couldn't stay in Jacksonville forever. We drove down to Jacksonville so I could get my things and wrap up some loose ends, and driving back to Savannah, with the St. Johns River in my rearview mirror, I felt an overwhelming sense of relief. No more drama with a dying indie rock scene in an armpit of a city. No more family problems. No more struggling to find jobs. There was nothing left but opportunity, and I was ready to seize it.

Indeed, it didn't take long to find a job in Savannah. There must be four restaurants on every block, and Lisa seemed to know everyone, so there were plenty of opportunities. The first one that bit was The Lady and Sons—yes, that one. I can't say that I'm proud of it now, but I was young, and Paula Deen had just gotten her first Food Network show, so it seemed like an opportunity then. I also saw a little bit of my mother in Paula at times—she was a single mom and she'd struggled before she made it big and her first restaurant, The Bag Lady, wasn't actually that much different from the Whistle Stop. Plus, I do fucking love fried chicken.

The kitchen at The Lady and Sons was huge, but otherwise, it wasn't any different from any other kitchen. The sous chef was fucking the general manager, one of the cooks sold pot to some of the staff, and Paula . . . Oh, Paula. She wasn't around much, but when she would breeze through, with a Virginia Slims cigarette in her hand, the only words I remember her saying were "fuck this," "fuck that," "butter," and "y'all." I thought I was bad, but she had the mouth of a French sailor. It was a far cry from the sugar-sweet, matronly persona she played on TV.

At the time, I was a pretty stand-up guy, which I kept thinking back to as I languished in New York, jumping from job to job, cheating on my girlfriend and fucking things up because I was too drunk or high to do my job. In Savannah, at first, it was I who was faithful and Lisa who cheated. I mostly let it slide because I was young and naïve, and after Lisa's lease ran out, we found a new place together, but it ate at me even though I wasn't willing to walk out. I worked hard, drank within reason, and I wasn't doing drugs. At least not yet.

Most of the time, when I was off work, we hung out at the same wine bar that Lisa had taken me to on my first night in Savannah. And pretty soon, I figured out what it was that had given me such a weird vibe: It was because Lisa only went there to cop cocaine. As did every other fucking person there.

I tried to ignore it at first, but one morning after a long night at the bar, Lisa told me that she had a surprise for me. It was close to dawn—bars close at three A.M. in Savannah, but sometimes, if you know the owner, they'll lock you in so you can stay all night—but Lisa was wired. She pulled out a gram of cocaine wrapped in plastic, forming a little thumbnail-size ball. For a minute, I was speechless. And then I was angrier than I'd ever been in my entire life.

Suddenly, a wave of memories came washing over me. My mother high or drunk, beating on and getting beat by her girlfriends. My mother wasting away her money and opportunities on the little white bags that floated in and out of our lives. I knew cocaine was to blame for everything that was wrong with my childhood, and I couldn't believe Lisa was doing it, and was offering it to me. Back at home, I yelled at her until I was red in the face, and spitting from the corners of my mouth. She put it in her jewelry box and we didn't talk about it again.

Meanwhile, though, I was getting bored with deep-frying at The Lady and Sons, and figured that I was nineteen years old and should learn some technique other than frying chicken, cooking grits, and torching crème brûlées. My first stop, though, wasn't much better—a "gourmet gas station" called Parker's. And I'm talking literally. In between cooking, I actually had to pump people's gas. What it did, though, was lead me to my next job. A regular customer used to come in with a chef's jacket on. One day, out of desperation, I asked if he knew anyone looking for cooks. He said he was, and within minutes, I'd turned in my squeegees and name tag and told him I'd be in the next day.

The new gig was a place called Savannah Bistro which was serving what they called French-Thai fusion with a Southern flair. I know, it's hokey as hell, but I was nineteen and desperate to learn, even if it came via clichés. They were known for their crispy flounder, which was fried whole and then smothered in a super-sweet apricot-shallot marmalade. The grouper in Thai barbecue sauce was much simpler—they just used vinegar, mushrooms, ketchup, spices, and aromatics—but it was much better. It was bistro food, really, and not much different from what I'd been doing in Jacksonville. But it was there that I got to work a line, put an occasional dish on the menu, learn some decent knife cuts, and make a livable wage.

In Savannah, too, I got my first real taste of what kitchen culture was like. It wasn't just Lisa who was doing coke. I mean, it was fucking everywhere. Every one of the chefs and line cooks was high as a kite both in and out of the kitchen. I continued to resist for a while, but one day, I came home from work tired and grumpy as hell. What could it really hurt to try it just one time?

"Fuck it," I said to Lisa, and told her to grab the cocaine.

To my surprise, it was right there in her jewelry box where she'd left it. She hadn't touched it since our fight. I was nervous and she got it out of the baggie, cut it up on a DVD case, and handed me a line. I hesitated.

"What will this do to me?" I asked. "Can I die from this?"

Lisa laughed. "Just go ahead and snort it."

And I did. I can still remember it as if it was yesterday—first it was a deep numbness that spread from my nasal cavity all the way to my right front tooth. And then the rush set in. We must have finished the gram in about an hour, alternating lines, and then we just attacked each other. We fucked for what must have been six hours. I had never experienced a high like that, or a climax so exquisite. I was hooked.

It didn't take me long to leave Lisa or Savannah after that, for the first time anyway. We started doing coke at least twice a week, and her cheating got even worse. After a few weeks, I got fed up and gave notice at Savannah Bistro, ready to head back to Jacksonville.

Although I left Georgia in a hurry, it had a considerable impact on me. Years later, in New York, I got I LOVE GA tattooed on my hand as a tribute to my roots. I suppose I missed Georgia, having spent many years in New York City, but I also wanted to keep a reminder of the South with me because I knew, deep down, that I would probably never return.

Like the tattoo across my hand, Georgia had left an indelible mark on me. It had given me cocaine.

∽

Four years had passed between Savannah and that first year in New York. I was twenty-three years old by then and thought I'd seen a lot—I'd been on my own since I was fifteen and toured the U.S. with Kylesa before I could even legally buy a drink. But New York is a whole different animal, and I was just beginning to scratch the surface of it.

Chloe had moved up to New York with me, and while our relationship had always been pretty volatile, it was like the city brought out every terrible impulse in both of us. We signed a lease together on a tiny one-bedroom in SoHo, which was necessary for financial reasons as much as anything else, but we were at each other's throats from day one, screaming at each other even as we were moving our bed up the dark, narrow stairwell to our apartment.

It isn't always easy to live with someone, and especially not in New York, where everything is smaller and more expensive and seemingly every temptation is literally around the corner. With only three hundred square feet between us, it felt like every time I was home, Chloe was in my face, red hair blazing, temper—and sometimes even fists—flaring up at me. She was deeply irrational, outrageously jealous, and, most of the time, just downright fucking mean, telling me I'd never amount to anything, that I was a piece of shit who'd never even finished high school, that I was nothing but an addict and a drunk, that I didn't deserve any of the chances I'd got-

ten, that every time I failed at a job, I deserved it. I'm not saying I was great to her, either. Far from it, in fact. But everything
she said to me was like a punch in the stomach, and every time
I came home, I wanted nothing more than to leave again, as
soon as possible.

So, instead of going home, I started hanging out after my
shift most nights at Motor City Bar on the Lower East Side, a
dark little dive with hubcap barstools, cheap drinks, a DJ
playing punk and metal and rockabilly, and sometimes even a
go-go dancer in the window—totally my kind of place. If I
wasn't there, I was at The Room on Sullivan Street in SoHo,
which was directly around the corner from my apartment on
Broome. On the surface, The Room didn't fit quite as much
with my personality, at least then—a little swankier, and more
intimate, with no hard liquor, but a long list of imported beer
and wine.

It was at The Room, though, where I got my first real
hookup—a tall, lanky dude named Borga who was probably
in his mid-forties, and looked like he'd slept through the last
three decades. He always wore bell-bottoms and midriff-
baring T-shirts, which went perfectly with his giant Afro.
When I first met Borga, he would sell me coke twisted up in
foil gum wrappers. Then, he started teaching me about one of
New York's classic services—cocaine delivery. It is the city
that never sleeps, for fuck's sake, where anything is only one
phone call away, no matter what time of night or day, and
drugs were no different. Anytime I wanted to score some coke
after that, I'd just go find Borga. He'd pick up the phone, hit
speed dial, and say: "Hey, Johnny, lemme get two pieces of

pie." A half hour later, sometimes even less, a silver Hyundai would pull up with a Dominican guy in the driver's seat. Borga would hop in the backseat for about forty-five seconds, come out, throw me a gram, then take off to the bar, and that was that. It was easier to score coke in New York than it was to order a goddamn pizza.

Whether I was at The Room or Motor City, once I'd gotten my delivery, I'd set my sights on finding a girl, which never seemed much harder, either, than calling Johnny for two slices of pie. I'd get high, follow the girl home, and fuck her senseless until the next morning, when I'd skulk back to my apartment on Broome Street to get some sleep on the couch. Sometimes I'd feel bad, seeing Chloe sleeping when I'd walk into the apartment. I'd try to apologize when she woke up, try to say it wouldn't happen again. But as soon as she'd open her mouth, I'd get indignant and scream right back at her. As meaningless, as mindless, as drug-fueled and stupid as whatever sex I'd just had was, it would somehow become ammunition—anything was better than being home with her.

It didn't take long before Chloe realized that two could play my game. We lived above a little French bistro called La Sirène, and Chloe started hanging out at the bar and pretty soon was fucking the cook, some douche-bag Parisian who used to come up to the apartment before I got home from work. I was pissed, even though I guess I didn't have much right to be, but Chloe's affair gave me even more freedom to do whatever the hell I wanted. Guilt-free, I pretty much started banging everything I met that had a vagina and weighed less than 140 pounds.

One early fall night, about a year and a half after I'd moved to New York, I was sitting at the bar at The Room late at night after a shift. I had just scored a gram and was about halfway through it by way of frequent trips to the bathroom, thinking about calling it a night, when a girl caught my eye. She was gorgeous, and much more my type than Chloe—short, Jewish-looking, with dark hair and a nice ass. I always played a game with myself where, if I looked over at a girl and made eye contact three times, I'd go in for the kill. This girl—her name was Genevieve—was a goner from the start, and a few beers later, we were out of there.

We couldn't go to my apartment, of course, since I shared it with Chloe, but Genevieve said she lived two blocks away, also on Broome Street, a lucky coincidence. We started walking over to her apartment, exactly one block east of mine, above Sam Mason's Tailor, the tension and anticipation growing with every step. Coke and adrenaline were pulsing through my veins in equal proportion, and I couldn't wait to get this girl home and into her bed.

As Genevieve was putting her key in the door, though, and turned to tell me something, I realized it was going to be a little more complicated than that. She didn't live alone either, she said—she bunked with a roommate, and she meant that literally; they slept in the same room, on bunk beds. I didn't think too much of it; we were in New York City for fuck's sake. People live by drastic means. But for a minute there, as she was telling me this in the doorway, I started to panic. I was more excited about this girl than I had been about anyone else in months. Was this all going to be just a giant tease?

But then she turned back around, grabbed my hand, and giggled drunkenly: "I do have a roof deck. . . ."

Within what felt like seconds, we were up on the roof, my pants were down, the rest of the cocaine was in our nostrils, and her mouth was around my dick. As I fucked her with half of her body hung over the ledge of 525 Broome Street, the fall sky stretched out above us and the city spread out like a blanket below, high on drugs and sex and everything else, I was in complete euphoria. This wild girl felt like the exact opposite of my nagging, bitchy girlfriend, and for a minute, with her, I felt like I could do anything. Maybe, I thought after we finished and lay stretched out, panting, on the rooftop, this girl was just the amount of crazy that I needed in my life.

Genevieve and I made plans to meet up a few days later, and those days felt like years. I couldn't stop thinking about that rooftop, and what she'd have in store for me next. But as soon as we met, Genevieve said that she had something to tell me.

As it turns out, she wasn't exactly the raging party girl I thought she was: She was a religious Jehovah's Witness who didn't drink or smoke, much less do coke on a rooftop with a complete stranger. And, before me, she hadn't had sex for six fucking years.

I couldn't believe what I was hearing, and as she talked, I went back over the night a million times in my mind. What had I said or done to this girl to make her stray so drastically from her life and her upbringing? How had we ended up on that rooftop together? To this day, I don't know. Maybe she was questioning things and I was the straw that broke some camel's back in her mind that night. Maybe she was just feeling particularly impulsive, as something brought her to The Room in the first place. Maybe I was her own personal Rum-springa, when Amish teenagers are encouraged to go out and experience the world before settling down. All I knew, and all I needed to know then, was that she'd felt something, too, that night, and she wanted to keep seeing me. And that's how I met the mother of my son.

CHAPTER FOUR

I've never been particularly religious. It wasn't a huge part of my upbringing, aside from a few hellish months when I lived with my father in Opelousas, Louisiana, as a teenager and was forced to go to a Catholic school. It was a bad time for me in general—since I was the product of a date rape, my parents really had no relationship with each other for most of my childhood. But when I was twelve, I decided I wanted a father. My mother obliged and sent me to Louisiana to live with him and his new wife and family, and their expectations of me were a little different than my mom's had been in Jacksonville. I went from skateboarding and drumming and hanging out all night with my friends in Florida to playing football at a Catholic school, for fuck's sake.

My father also had something to do with the other reason that I've always rejected religion: because it preaches the idea of forgiveness. Obviously, I know what it's like to make mistakes and to get second chances. I wouldn't be here if I didn't. But the idea that anything can be forgiven doesn't sit well with me. I hold grudges, and the biggest one I hold goes back my entire life—to my father, which started the day I was born.

As apathetic as I was about religion, though, Genevieve was the opposite. She had been raised her whole life in an insular community of Jehovah's Witnesses in Nevada City, California, and had moved to New York to go to school and become a hairstylist. And when we first started dating, I started to wonder if maybe she was on to something. Not that I was finding Jesus or anything, but I did feel like, once I met her, I hit my first stroke of luck since I'd moved to New York. There was a feeling of acceptance I got from Genevieve, which was probably a vestige of her former life in Nevada City.

By the time I met Genevieve, shit had officially hit the fan with Chloe. I'd known that it was over for months at that point, but until then, I'd never had the impetus to do anything about it. Sure, I was a cheating bastard. But I knew how to play the field. I never cared enough about anyone else to do anything about it, and no one stuck around long enough to add enough fuel to Chloe's fire either. As long as I was still on a lease with Chloe, I stood my ground and kept living there. I may have been sleeping on the couch, but at least it was a place to sleep.

I hated the way I was when I was with Chloe, especially because I knew deep down that I was starting to echo some of the shitty relationships I'd seen my mother in when I was a kid. My mother has been happily married for over a decade now to a wonderful woman named Carline, a woman I've come to think of as just as much a mother as my own. But before they met, my mother was definitely a ladies' woman, jumping from one abusive, degrading relationship to another.

The earliest one I can remember was a woman named Debra, a jealous, angry bitch of a woman whom my mother started seeing when I was around five years old, and they would fight like motherfuckers. I know when most people think of women fighting, it's all slapping and biting and scratching at each other with nails. This wasn't like that. I'm talking actual fistfights, night after night after night. We were living then in a brick quadplex directly behind the high school from which I'd later drop out, and there was a family of squirrels living on the roof. Every night, I'd lie in bed and listen to them run around, imagining that they were Alvin and the Chipmunks, and that they were having an exciting adventure right above my head. It was what I did to drown out the yelling and the thumps from my mom and Debra rolling around and fighting on the floor below me.

My mom and Debra split up when I was around eight, and we moved into a new apartment with a new girlfriend. Her name was Lisa, and she was fat and jowly with a kind of pompadour haircut. Think Cam from *Modern Family*, but a woman. To this day, I don't know what my mom saw in her. She claimed to be an artist, but she wasn't talented—she painted shit like giraffes, but on tiles. With acrylic. They were completely tacky. She wasn't attractive. She was mean to me. And the fighting was even worse than it had been with Debra. This time, though, I wasn't just a little kid anymore, and I wasn't up in my bed, hoping Alvin would come and save me. I was fiercely protective of my mom, and one night, in the middle of a particularly bad fight, I ran into the kitchen and grabbed a knife, jumping in and waving it in Lisa's face. It was a shock to everyone involved, but an effective way to end a fight. I'm not violent by nature, but something in me had snapped. And I have always been good with a knife, a pride of many chefs.

I never wanted my own relationships to be like my mother's, but with Chloe, I could see myself going down that path. And maybe Genevieve gave me an excuse to do it. To this day, I'm not exactly sure what was different about Genevieve than any of the other girls. What it was about her that finally made me get off my ass. The chemistry was just on with her, and at the beginning, we couldn't get enough of each other. Plus, there was the fact that she had essentially given up everything she'd been raised to believe in, just to be with me. I didn't quite understand, but it was incredibly flattering.

Things finally seemed like they were going to look up in my professional life, too. I'd been bouncing around from kitchen to kitchen, not quite finding the right fit when, a few weeks after I met Genevieve, I got hooked up with a pretty sweet gig: lead cook/tournant at a little speakeasy bar called Employees Only.

It was a good time for speakeasies in New York—there was Milk & Honey on the Lower East Side, where you had to find an unlisted number to make a reservation, and PDT in the East Village, which you could only get to by entering through a telephone booth in the hot-dog stand next door. It's

like they say in *Swingers*: All the cool bars have to be hard to
find and have no sign. Employees Only wasn't actually that
hard to find—it was on Hudson Street, in the West Village—
but you did have to know about it, and there wasn't a sign. Or
anyway a sign that had anything to do with the actual estab-
lishment. There was a green awning with a key-shaped sym-
bol, a little *EO* on the door, and, in the window in glowing
red neon, letters that spelled out *PSYCHIC*.

Inside, EO did everything they could to keep up the Prohi-
bition theme: a heavy, velvet curtain at the front door, red
leather banquettes, and low lighting. Bartenders were dressed
like goodfellas—I'm talking three-piece suits and fedoras every night—and they served up the most perfect Manhattans
and old-fashioneds (along with some more contemporary
spins) I'd ever had.

EO was primarily a bar, but they were also doing some
really decent food. The woman who hired me was named Julia, who's still the executive chef there, and I remember her
keeping a super-organized kitchen, and turning out some
good dishes. The food was simple—at dinner we did a roasted
chicken, a skirt steak, a few kinds of fish, things like that—
but it was well put together. Given that it was primarily a bar,
they were better known for their late-night menu, which was
served from midnight until three thirty A.M. Most of it was
basic bar food with an expensive edge, like Wagyu burgers
with truffle fries, and oysters on the half shell. But they did
have one thing on the menu that I loved—a staff meal that,
like the real thing, changed every night based on what the
kitchen had around. Anyone who's ever worked in a restau-

rant gets the importance of staff meal, or family meal, but I'm sure it never crosses the minds of most customers when they sit down to eat.

At family meals, the staff isn't usually eating a perfectly plated Wagyu burger, or sucking down an oyster on the half shell. In most restaurants, the staff just makes use of whatever extra food is lying around, plus some items like pasta or rice that they buy specifically for staff. At some places, every chef de partie makes something from their station. Usually that means that the garde manger is responsible for something cold, the fish cook would prepare extra from his entremets, the meat cook would use trimmings or scraps like roast duck wings, the pastry cooks would make a simple cake. It varies a lot from restaurant to restaurant.

At Alinea, the daytime commis chefs were responsible for cooking family meal, and the entire meal was bought in for the staff. You could never predict what it would be—tacos one day, stir-fry the next. At Schwa the chef, Michael Carlson, would make food for us, and it was the best family meal of anywhere I've worked. He would make chilaquiles one day, the next morning he would make biscuits and gravy, and then after dinner service he'd take us to Korean BBQ, where we would drink Korean soju and grill short ribs at our own table to pair with the thirty-plus condiments that were scattered about. I hear Per Se has a theme every day, like deli day and pizza day. I think every chef takes a different approach to it. I loved that EO put that right out there for the customers, too, like it was inviting them into our world, giving them literally a taste of what it meant to work in food.

Even though it wasn't really expanding my culinary hori-
zons, and even though the hours were backbreakingly long
(the dangers of bar work—our shifts lasted from twelve P.M.
to one A.M., when a second crew came in to finish the late
menu shift and a second cleanup), it was a good gig for a couple of reasons. First, they were paying me nine hundred dollars a week, some over and under the table, which was pretty
solid for what I was doing. And second, I got along well with
people there. At first, I definitely held my head a little high.
The gap between me and the other cooks was wide—I'd been
in much higher positions at better restaurants—and everyone
knew it. But once I shut the hell up, I worked well with Julia
and her sons, and I immediately hit it off with one of the servers, this skinny dude named Tommy, who quickly became a
good friend.

Tommy was a little older than me, and a career waiter
with a shared interest in my favorite drug. He was a good
guy—really good, actually—and he was clearly happy to have
someone around to hang out with after a shift. At the end of
one of my first nights working there, he showed up in the
kitchen and slipped me an FO matchbook, and when I opened
it, there was a gram of coke inside. As we got to be friends,
that became somewhat a ritual. His shift ended later than
mine, so when I was done, I'd hang out at the bar and get
some drinks if I had the cash, and Tommy and I would pass
the blow back and forth until he got off his shift. Sometimes
Julia would join me in drinking, and she'd order us whiskey
gingers and we'd shoot the shit. It was no Le Bernardin, but
for work, I have to say, it wasn't so bad.

I'd been working at EO for about three weeks when one morning, I rolled up for my noon shift to a big fucking surprise. The restaurant wasn't open yet, so the doors were still locked, but sitting right out in front of them, for all the world to rifle through, was every single fucking thing I owned. We're talking duffel bags of clothes, garbage bags full of CDs, books, everything I'd been lugging around with me since I was fifteen.

My jaw literally dropped, and I just stood there, in the middle of Hudson Street looking like a cartoon version of *The Scream* or Macaulay Culkin in *Home Alone*, staring at all my worldly possessions turned into what could quickly become a flea market for the bums of the West Village. I wasn't surprised, exactly. I hadn't moved out of the apartment I shared with Chloe, but I'd been seeing Genevieve pretty consistently for the last three weeks, which meant I basically hadn't been coming home at night. Genevieve's bunk-bed situation made it impossible to sleep there, but with my newfound cash flow, we'd usually hit up some cheap motel room, or figure out something else. I guess, I thought as I cursed her very existence at the top of my lungs, this meant that Chloe and I were finally done. I was starting to gather things, slinging a duffel over my shoulder and picking up one of the trash bags, when the door to EO swung open from the inside. It was Julia, buttoning up her chef's coat and looking sympathetic.

"She called here, too, you know," Julia said.

Of course she had. The first job I had in a year that I actually liked, and that crazy bitch was going to fuck it all up.

"I bet she did," I called back. "What's the verdict?"

"Oh, she ranted and raved for a long time. Said you were a crackhead and that I was wasting my time with you."

"Yeah, that sounds about right."

"Is that true?"

"The crackhead part? It was. But I don't do that anymore," I said, thinking of the gram of coke that Tommy and I had put away the night before. But it was true, at least in the most literal sense; it wasn't crack.

Julia nodded and started to go back inside.

"Do I still have a job?" I called after her.

"Of course. Hurry up with all that crap and get in here. Plenty to do."

I breathed a little easier and followed Julia into the bar. But that didn't solve the larger problem: Where the fuck was I supposed to live? I couldn't stay with Genevieve, given her roommate situation, and even though I'd been in New York for a while at that point, things with work and Chloe had been so volatile that I hadn't made the kinds of close friends that would just let me move in on a whim. As the panic was starting to well up in my stomach, I felt a reassuring hand on my shoulder. It was Tommy: steady, calm, kind Tommy.

"I heard what happened, dude," he said, picking up a trash bag filled with my crap. "Don't worry about it. You'll stay with me." I couldn't believe my luck. And for a minute there, it really felt like everything was going to be okay. Tommy lived in the Kensington section of Brooklyn, kind of a random neighborhood south of Prospect Park, inhabited by probably the most mixed assortment of religions and cultures

I had ever seen, but he had a comfortable apartment, way bigger than the shoe box in SoHo that I'd grown used to.

Now that we had a place to go, too, I was spending every night with Genevieve. Usually she'd show up at the end of a shift, while I was drinking and waiting for Tommy. We'd go back to Kensington, do blow, drink beer, and listen to Tommy play covers of The Who on the mandolin. Then, finally, Genevieve and I would retire, which usually meant staying up and doing more blow and fucking until the sun came up and I had to get ready to go back to work and do it all again. It wasn't sustainable, but shit, it was fun.

One Saturday night, Genevieve came to pick me up and we stayed around and drank with Julia for a while, who asked me to be her new sous when the current one left. I was psyched and feeling like things were finally smooth sailing. Julia went home, but Genevieve and I stayed out, met up with some new friends we had just made, and things got a little crazier and later than I'd expected. It was a typical Saturday night, but in the midst of all of it, I completely forgot about a seven thirty brunch shift I had the next morning. I overslept and woke up hours later, still a little geeked out, to a phone full of messages from Julia.

It wasn't the first time I'd slept through a shift at a restaurant job, and it certainly wouldn't be the last. But the EO family had been so good to me that the guilt was palpable. I probably could've owned up to Julia, begged for another chance, and kept my job. But I knew I'd screwed up, badly, and I just couldn't face her. Plus, in the haze of my hangover, I vaguely remembered Julia saying that I could be the sous at her new restaurant. This was going to be bad, but I'd land on my feet again, somehow.

The sous job never materialized, of course. And, to make matters worse, when Tommy found out what had happened with EO and Julia, he told me, in the most polite and kind way possible, that it was time for me to grow the fuck up, and asked me to leave.

Leaving EO and Tommy's apartment, I felt like a dog with my tail stuffed so far between my legs I couldn't walk. I knew I'd had something good, and once again, I'd squandered it. I was so embarrassed that I didn't even pick up any of my things from Tommy. I just shoved everything I could into one duffel, and left, saying I'd be back the next day to get it. I never saw him again.

I walked to the Ditmas stop on the F train from Tommy's apartment. My gray duffel was stuffed to the brim with a couple of books, about a quarter of my wardrobe, a pair of white-and-brown low-top Pumas, and a pair of Sanita clogs for cooking. On my other arm I had a tote with more books and my knife roll. It was all I could physically carry. I wasn't sure where I was going. All I knew is that I was hungover as fuck and Genevieve was by my side.

The twenty-minute train ride back to SoHo seemed like three hours, and it was the last place I wanted to be after a night of cocaine abuse. Any public place with people you don't know is the last place you want to be. Any unfamiliar face is frightening. You become hypersensitive to light: Imagine coming out of a 3-D matinee at two P.M., and you can't even open your eyes. In addition, paranoia sets in, you begin to believe everyone around you is staring at you. You create their thoughts in your head. And you believe them.

In between all my crazy thoughts, though, I needed to find a place to stay. Genevieve said she would talk to her roommate about me crashing for a day or two, but we both already knew that wouldn't go over very well with her Watchtower friend.

In the meantime, I figured I'd go to the Bowery and check into my favorite hotel, a shitty Korean place where you could get a room for sixty bucks and a twenty-dollar deposit. They also would check your ID so they could file a police report if you stole something, which would be pretty hard to do, since the only thing in the room was a rock-hard twin bed.

Genevieve and I sat in the hotel room for three days and three nights, trying to figure out what to do next. We ate nothing but Adderall—sweet little orange gelcaps filled with tiny sugarcoated pebbles that made sure we didn't get hungry for anything else. We walked around Chinatown at all the hours of the night, aimless and completely fucked up.

On the third night, the hallucinations began to set in. I'd been awake for close to a week straight, and I couldn't distinguish my imagination from reality. I became completely horrified of Chloe, even though I hadn't seen her in weeks. The thought of running into her scared the living shit out of me. She was physically harmless, but I thought that she could figure out a way—just a few life-altering words that would come out of her throat and skip across her lips—to tarnish my reputation even further by pulling the same shit she had weeks earlier with Julia at EO. I asked myself that a lot, too. Who was Chloe contacting, to get back at me for the pain I caused her? In my head, it could have been anyone. Anyone and everyone. The damage she had done to my career is in no way close to the terror I spread with my constant anxiety—like a hurricane of shit. But I still had fear in my heart for what I thought she could do. I started shaking anytime I saw any person that resembled her. Even in the slightest of ways.

My money started to run out around this time, and I knew I had to figure out another solution. I thought about my options, which seemed sparse. I still hadn't been in the city that long. I knew a lot of people, but knowing people in New York doesn't count for much. Spare bedrooms don't really exist. So there I was, with two bags and a knife roll. Nowhere to go. I thought about a shelter, but I wasn't quite at that point yet. Instead, I moved from the shitty Korean hotel to an even shittier hostel uptown on Amsterdam. Genevieve would come by in the evenings and we would hang out briefly and go have a couple of drinks somewhere and then she'd throw me some of her Adderall prescription when she left. As paranoid as I was in the Bowery, though, it only got worse in the hostel. I still wasn't sleeping at all, and was totally weirded out by the fact that I was sharing a room with twenty people I didn't know.

I've had some bad benders in my day, but that one was particularly rough, and looking back, I'm not entirely sure how I survived it. I was dangerously skinny—I couldn't have weighed more than 130 pounds—and jaundiced. I was wearing a lot of fedoras and suits at that time, and they were hanging off me as if my bones were made of wire. I went a week without food, a couple of days without water. I washed my drugs down with nothing but whiskey.

Near the end, when I finally ran out of cash, Genevieve did something I never thought she would do: She gave her roommate an ultimatum, telling her childhood friend that she could either deal with me living there or move out, knowing full well what her friend would pick. She left that very same night. I had no idea what was going on. In retrospect, I should have known that it would go down like that. I had a fucking pentagram tattooed on my stomach. What choice did her roommate even have? Abandon her beliefs? Let someone she thought was full of evil spirits cohabit with her? It's something I didn't think of at all at the time. I just thought she was a judgmental bitch. The thing was, if anyone was judgmental, it was me. I hadn't thought of the fact that the girl was brought up in this religion, not really knowing anything else. They lived within their community, only ever leaving that community to cold-call non-believers.

Spending time with Genevieve, who was raised to believe that it was not only right to push your beliefs on others but it was your duty, made me think about the concept of proselytizing in general. At the time, I was sickened by it. And speaking only in terms of religion, I still take issue with the idea of it. Late teens and early twenties is not an age when people are particularly inclined to accept the beliefs of others, and that was especially true for me. Being told what to believe by an absent father who sent me to Catholic school, then told by my girlfriend that I was a piece of shit who'd never amount to anything, made it difficult to swallow anyone else's opinion on any topic. But recently, I began to wonder how that same concept applied to what I do every day.

When you think about it, all chefs are, in essence, spending every day pushing their beliefs on others. Food beliefs, to me, are no different from spiritual beliefs. Serving someone something to eat is a way to show them how you believe they should eat. I've come to the conclusion that this form of proselytizing is very different from the kind that's done with religious intent. With so many possible techniques and flavor profiles that more or less depend on the ethnic background of any given food, I see our work in the kitchen more as a forum. It can get catty depending on the egos involved, but at the core it's based on a mutual respect of the subject at hand: food. I'm pretty sure all cooks can agree that we respect all types of food, which is more than certain religious groups can say about accepting one another's version of an all-powerful god. I'm also pretty damn sure that a disagreement on food preparation was never the catalyst of a global war. So now I guess I can say that, if you believe in something, you should be able to share it with others. If it happens to inconvenience you, oh, well. At least you can tell someone to fuck off without fear that they'll knock your lights out.

Moving in to Genevieve's apartment was pretty easy: When the roommate left, I walked in. The last few weeks had made me whittle my worldly possessions down to a duffel, a box, and a knife roll, so it didn't take much for me to settle in. I figured that we would disassemble the bunk beds now that the roommate wasn't there anymore, but pretty soon, our domestic scene got another participant: a drug dealer friend of mine named Neo who was there so often, it just made sense to leave up the other bed.

I initially met Neo through Craigslist, which, shockingly, is a pretty common practice. It's all out there in the open, on the Internet, for everyone to see. But for most drug dealers I know, that's how they find their first clients. Of course, there's an intricate system of code, but the people who are searching for this catch on pretty quickly. I mean, who doesn't know what "420" means? Or how does the guy who says he's looking for ski lift tickets in the middle of July in Manhattan not get pegged for a cokehead?

I guess I was just as stupid as all the rest of these Craigslist fucks when I met Neo—but in fairness, I was in a desperate place. When I moved in with Genevieve, I didn't have a job—getting fired from EO was what had set the whole disastrous chain of events in motion—and I didn't have any prospects for a job, either. It's safe to say that I was in a bit of a panic. For the first time since my mom told me on my seventeenth birthday that I always needed to have a backup plan, I found myself without one. I started scanning the Internet manically, sending out resumes to almost every listing I could find. I was totally freaking out. I figured that I probably could survive for ten more days without getting a job, and those ten days felt like the longest of my life. Day One went by and I said I'd be sure to hear from someone tomorrow. Day Two went by and I blamed it on the weekend. "No one calls new hires on Friday. I'll have to wait till Monday," I said. Days Three and Four went by. I was getting increasingly panicked. Finally, on Day Eight, the phone rang. It was Susan Wine, ex-wife of Barry

Wine, chef and owner of The Quilted Giraffe, named one of the most important restaurants in the U.S. due to its nouvelle cuisine style, and it was ahead of its time in emphasizing foraged and homegrown produce.

When Susan asked for me, I immediately sparked up. I knew it. This was it. She was going to offer me a job. I didn't care what job it was. As long as it paid money, we were going to be okay. Especially if it meant not relying on dealing drugs with Neo to keep afloat. Genevieve had been fired from her job at the salon about a month earlier and spent her days sitting on the couch doing fuck all. It was crucial that I get a job.

It turned out that the restaurant was Wine Bar at Vintage, and I was stoked to find out that it was only three blocks from my new apartment. I quickly showered, put on some decent-looking clothes, and trucked it straight to Wooster and Broome. The interview was downstairs in their cellar, which was also where the kitchen was. And the private dining room. And the restrooms. And the offices. The place was gigantic. Not just by New York City standards, either. It was big.

Susan's last chef was a lot like me—a hopper who moved from job to job, and he'd only lasted four months. She was pretty eager to replace him, and twenty minutes later, I walked out as the new chef. I got a $55,000 salary and was told I could do whatever food I wanted as long as I only used product from the state of New York, which was part of their whole shtick. That and, as the name implied, their wine list. They had more than two hundred bottles, which they offered by both the bottle and the glass. Given that a week ago, I'd been basically homeless, not knowing what my next move would be, this seemed like a pretty good place to land. It was like showing up at Nora's, but being presented with a much larger toolbox.

Settling into Vintage was pretty easy and comfortable, especially because they had a sous chef set up already, a Polish immigrant who had been in New York only for a few months. She knew English well and she already knew how to cook. The first time I met her, though, I was a little surprised. She was wearing your typical clogs and chef pants, but there was something different about her porter shirt. She had only buttoned half of it and was wearing it as a midriff, baring her stomach. But I always thought that if she had the balls to dress like that in a kitchen, then I might as well let her. It didn't hurt that she was attractive, too.

But Justyna wasn't solely eye candy. She was awesome to work with, and our relationship turned out to be the most mutually enriching experience I've ever had with a sous. She taught me things she learned in Poland, like how to make a perfect pierogi. It didn't end there, though. She taught me things that an American wouldn't know, like horseradish and beef tongue, for instance. She always boiled beef tongue with horseradish. Not only do the flavors meld well, but the allyl isothiocyanate (a chemical in horseradish) helps the skin peel easier from the flesh. Did Justyna know what causes the allyl isothiocyanate reaction in the tongue? Hell, no. But that's how her mom did it and that was enough for her.

Vintage turned out to be an awesome gig. Susan and her partner, Robert Ransom, were totally dedicated to using local, entirely New York product, which meant that we shopped only two places—the Union Square Farmers Market on Wednesdays and Fridays, and a middleman called Farm to Chef on Thursdays. They were sort of a mobile farmers' market, which meant that they purchased product directly from hundreds of farmers in the area and then delivered it all straight to me and other restaurants. On the other days, we had to fudge our product a bit—going to Chinatown and even cheating by using Nova Scotia lobster in our lobster rolls.

The result of all this was that I was using product comparable to what I'd seen at Nora—everything was fresh and completely in season. But the downside is that it was extremely expensive. I doubt if I ever came in under 41 percent for food cost the entire time that I worked there, which is, unfortunately, probably why the restaurant is now closed. Susan and Robert also owned a winery, just upstate on the Shawangunk Wine Trail in New Paltz, and much of the wine was sourced from there. Thanks to archaic zoning laws, though, the winery is now closed, too.

The best part about working at Vintage Wine Bar, aside from the product, was the amount of freedom that Susan gave me. The kitchen staff was tiny—just me, Justyna, and two deaf-mute dishwashers, so I basically could do whatever the fuck I wanted. Justyna and I were almost always on the same page, but more important, the fact that there wasn't anyone looking over my shoulder let me hone my technique without embarrassment or fear of doing it wrong.

A big part of what I taught myself during that chapter of my makeshift culinary school was about proteins. We got most of our proteins through Farm to Chef, and they delivered us essentially whole animals. They were butchered already, but we got every single part of the animal. By then, I had used every piece of every animal at one point in my life. But for most everything but the standard cuts, I'd used each of them only one time. Needless to say, it was good to have room to experiment. In addition to serving tongue, heart, liver, and kidneys, we also served kitschy things like Long Island duck meatballs paired with a charred tomato coulis, fingerling-potato-and-black-truffle pierogi with smoked paprika crème fraîche, and New York–style cheesecake blintz with Concord grape gastrique. Our goal was to represent New York in small plates.

The service staff at Vintage was mostly made up of theatre folk—one guy was in an episode of *The Sopranos*, and the rest were stage actors. They were all young and didn't have a lick of fine dining experience among them, but it was a tight-knit crew. Everyone drank at the bar when their shift was done, and when that got old, we moved on to another bar, usually Toad Hall on Grand, where we would drink whiskey and beer and shoot pool. Toad Hall was the main "industry bar" for the SoHo area. Cooks from Tailor, P*ong, Babbo, and wd~50 would go there after their shift and shoot the shit and bust one another's balls. I never saw a fight at Toad Hall; it was just a chill, laid-back environment to blow off steam after a shift.

So, for just a few months, it felt like things were smooth sailing. On the whole, I was happy with Genevieve and happy with work and it seemed like we might be getting by. But that must have been the calm before the storm, because pretty soon our worlds were turned upside down: Genevieve was pregnant.

At first, of course, I was in shock. And then I was nervous. I mean, incredibly nervous. This was new to me, and neither Genevieve nor I had any idea what we were getting into. But my reaction after that surprised even me: I wasn't upset about the pregnancy. In fact, I was excited. And even though I had no idea how we were going to do it, all I knew was that I was going to do my damnedest to be a good father. A great father. A father in every way unlike my own. My son wouldn't have to be taught to shave, use a condom, or protect his family by a highway truck–driving uncle he only saw once a year.

If that was my plan, though, I wasn't off to the best start. I was still using drugs, and so was Genevieve. And, maybe even worse, I was selling them, too. Nothing hard—just some weed here and there with Neo, the dealer I'd met on Craigslist. As much as I knew that it was risky, we also didn't have much of a choice. Genevieve had lost her job, and while I had a steady salary from Vintage, it wasn't enough to cover our $2,000-a-month rent.

At that point, it had been nearly three years since I'd seen my mother. The last time I saw her, I'd been driving home for Easter from Savannah and had gotten pulled over for speeding, which could have been particularly bad since I didn't have a license. The officer had a thick, Lowcountry accent and dark black sunglasses and I was scared shitless. But, after asking me if my tattoos were gang-related, he surprised me and asked where I was headed. I told him home and he asked how long it had been since I'd seen the woman who raised me.

Then he let me go. "It's Easter, after all," he said. "But drive the speed limit."

When she found out that Genevieve was pregnant, my mom decided that she ought to end the streak and come visit me in New York for the first time. She wanted to meet Genevieve, who would soon be the mother of her grandchild, and the timing worked out so that she would be there the week of my twenty-third birthday. It was winter in New York, the year that Heath Ledger died just a few blocks from our apartment. We were all together that morning, watching his body get wheeled out of his loft on Broome Street, like some sort of ominous warning about the shit that was about to come.

Genevieve was about four months pregnant, but things weren't going well. She wasn't drinking alcohol, but she did continue to smoke weed. So much that I had to stop leaving my stash at home for fear that when I got back from work, an eighth would be gone. We smoked a lot during the three days my mother was with us. We'd light up during the day, then walk around the city. I showed my mother the World Trade Center, or what was left of it. We went to bars and out to eat and spent a lot of time back at the apartment, just hanging out and talking about the future.

It was a future that none of us saw. I was getting increasingly stressed about being able to pay the bills, especially with the baby coming, but I dealt with it poorly—by turning over and over again to drugs. It was spiraling out of control, reaching levels that I hadn't seen maybe since DC, maybe ever before. The more I did drugs, the more Genevieve got scared. And the more she got scared, the more she started smoking weed, and then doing coke, and rounding it off with alcohol.

Finally, I pushed Genevieve to her breaking point. I'd disappeared for a week, cooped up with some random girl, doing cocaine and having sex for days on end, when I got a voice mail that simply said: "I'm leaving."

I went back home immediately, but there wasn't anything I could do about it. She was going back home to Nevada City, and I didn't have a leg to stand on. I had fucked up, royally this time, and I was also barely scraping by and had nothing to offer her or our future child. As we stood on the street saying good-bye, with me clutching a bag full of my clothes, I looked into her eyes and saw pure disappointment. I had let her down, in the worst way possible. We both cried, and as I wiped my face, I looked up. About a hundred feet down the street was a woman staring straight at us. I would later find out that the woman was Genevieve's mother. She was already there. Genevieve was already packed. And that exchange was the last physical contact I had with the mother of my son.

Genevieve leaving had been a wake-up call for me, and I knew I needed to make some changes in my life. It all suddenly hit me. I had been high for too long, I had disappointed people who truly cared about me, and I had nothing to show for the last year of my life. I had nowhere to live and no one to turn to. At this point, though, it wasn't so much about Genevieve as it was about my unborn child.

For the first few months after Genevieve left, my mother and I got some updates about the pregnancy. But during the last three months of the pregnancy, there was an abrupt change in what we were hearing from California. Instead of talking about visitation and child support, suddenly Genevieve told us that I was never to have contact with my own son, and in return, she wanted nothing from me.

I guess some guys would've felt they'd gotten off the hook, but I couldn't think of worse news. And there was nothing I could do about it. She was on the other side of the country, and I had no money to hire an attorney. I begged and pleaded with her not to cut me out of my own child's life, and she hung up on me. After that, all of my calls went unanswered and unreturned. With her silence, she sent a message loud and clear.

For all the bad times I had been through, this was one of the worst. All I had wanted was to be a better man than my father, and now I felt I had failed in exactly the same way. There was nothing I could do for my son. And the fact that Genevieve didn't want child support made it even worse. It made me useless. I didn't have much money, but I would have given whatever I had to him. Now she didn't even want that.

When she was eight months pregnant, Genevieve called my mom and told her that the baby was a boy and would be born on August 11. That was the last that my mom or I heard pertaining to Genevieve or to my child. It wasn't for lack of trying, either. I tracked down a salon in Nevada City where Genevieve was listed as a color specialist on their website. I called and asked for her on her day off, explaining that it was extremely urgent. But even though I left a fake name, the 917 area code must have given it away. I called back a week later and she "no longer worked there." All of the trails I had to find her and my son were cold.

My son will be five years old in August of 2013, and I don't know anything about him. I've never seen a picture of him, and I don't know his name. He probably has a new dad by now, and honestly, that's the best thing I can hope for, that he has a dad who's good to him in a way that mine never was to me. Because that's the only thing I can conjure up in my head to give me a little bit of peace.

CHAPTER FIVE

After Genevieve left, I found myself, yet again, at a crossroads, and the options looked pretty fucking bleak. In the haze of everything that had happened with the pregnancy and the drug binges, I hadn't been able to focus on work and had lost my job at Vintage. And with no income and no Genevieve, that also meant I had no place to live. There were three things I could do: I could go back to Florida and live with my mom, her wife, and her wife's mother. I could give in and live on the streets. Or I could call Chloe.

It's a bad sign when every fiber in my body was telling me that I'd be better off on the streets than with my ex-girlfriend, and to this day, I still don't know what possessed either of us to think this could possibly turn out okay. But I made the call, and reluctantly, she let me move back in. From the start, it wasn't a good situation. We weren't exactly back together, and I was sleeping on the couch most nights. And we still fought like banshees. Worse, even. I mean we really duked it out sometimes. She'd punch and slap me, and I'd get so angry that all I could do was push her into something. Usually, it was into a seated position on a couch. But somehow we kept it up for the next six months.

The only good thing that had come of the whole disaster with Genevieve, though, is that it made me seriously reconsider some of the other choices I was making in my life, and headed me, at least for a little while, on a path toward getting help. It wouldn't be the first time, and it definitely wouldn't be the last, but at that point, it was something.

I wasn't sure where to turn first. I'd always hated twelve-step programs, which I'd tried in South Carolina, Georgia, and DC. But I didn't have all that much to lose. And I was feeling desperate. I thought to myself that if the worst thing I had to do was make myself believe in some sort of higher power and in return I wouldn't want to use drugs anymore, then why the hell not?

The first thing I found was an AA meeting called Midnight Group, which was different in a few ways from other groups I'd been to. Instead of meeting in a church basement, like most of the others, Midnight Group had its own physical space. It was open twenty-four hours a day, and they hosted a meeting every hour on the hour. Another major difference is that most of the group leaders weren't from the city—they came in from suburbs, and then once they'd made connections with people in the city, they'd invite them to come out to their respective home group meetings. If that seems like a subtle difference to someone not well acquainted with programs, it's not. The Jersey leaders, unlike any others I'd known, were completely dominated by the Catholic Church. Every meeting I'd ever been to elsewhere ended with the Serenity Prayer. It's just standard practice. But in the Morristown group, we ended with the Catholic Our Father.

I first showed up to Midnight Group at eleven P.M. on a Friday. It was warm outside, which I remember distinctly because the place was packed. I'm not sure what it is about the cycle of addiction, but it seems like, in the winter, people tend to check into rehabs for treatment. When it's warm, they go to twelve-step meetings.

That night, about eight people from the Morristown Group were running the show. They were all young and excited—borderline aggressive, even. But I was immediately weirded out by their clothes. Every single one of them was wearing a tie and a button-up, collared shirt. It's pretty common knowledge among meeting goers I've encountered that the only people in ties and collared shirts are attorneys, coming straight from court. I mean, you're usually sitting around in an old, smelly, run-down, hundred-degree basement, for fuck's sake. Not exactly time for your Sunday best.

I was introduced to a guy named Matt, who welcomed me and handed me a Big Book, which is pretty much the bible of Alcoholics Anonymous. It's a balance of the organization's history, principles, and steps to recoveries and of inspirational stories from recovering addicts. I'd seen it before, but I just thanked him and accepted it.

They invited me to come back the next night, and with one day of sobriety under my belt, I was eligible to speak at the meeting. But there was something about the vibe that was rubbing me the wrong way. By the end of the night, they had invited me out to Morristown to attend their home group, which meant getting outfitted in a suit and tie that they lent me to be presentable at the church where the meeting was held. I went, in large part because they were so aggressive that I was worried they would follow me home and kidnap me. Apart from the clothes and the emphasis on religion, it wasn't all that different from other meetings that I'd been to. But I could tell from the start that these weren't my people. And having them spend the night trying to convince me that the only way I was going to get sober was to leave the city and crash on one of their couches ended up having the exact opposite effect. I decided even before I left that I would never be back.

Midnight Group got me all of three days clean, and then I turned to Narcotics Anonymous (NA), which seemed to be a little more my speed. The people there were less religious, definitely not dressed in suits and ties, and just generally seemed to get me and my experiences better. I wasn't going regularly but enough to remind myself that it was out there. And, with no money left in my pocket, I was ready to start my job search again.

I spent the next few months in and out of both restaurants and meetings in a vicious, never-ending cycle. I'd stick to the meetings, gather up a few months clean, and actually hold a job for a bit. And then one of them would fall apart, and it would all topple over. I'd relapse, quit or get fired, abandon the meetings, and start it all over again.

Only two of the jobs really stood out in my mind. The first was a place called Smith's, which was just opening on MacDougal Street, that hired me as their hot app cook—not ideal after some of the other positions that I'd held, but I needed the money, so it would have to do.

The chef was a tiny man named Pablo with an expensive chef jacket, a manicured goatee, and glasses. He had an impressive resume—he and his sous chef, Javier, were both poached from Bouley, where they both worked under César Ramirez, who is now famous for running Brooklyn's only Michelin three-starred restaurant, the Chef's Table at Brooklyn Fare. But despite his pedigree, Pablo was hardly an inspiring mentor. I picked up one trick from him—using transglutaminase to glue fish into roulades for more consistent butchering. But otherwise, it didn't seem he did all that much at all.

The food at Smith's was relatively simple, and it did turn out to be a good foundation later in my career, because it was the first time I had worked closely with any kind of modern techniques, like foams, gels, sous vide, and transglutaminase. There was one particular dish that stuck in my head—a polenta dish with an Arzak-style truffled egg and gorgonzola bubbles. It tasted great, even though, honestly, it smelled like a fart, and every night when I went home and thought about it, it made me sick. But it was pretty high concept for me at the time, with a popular technique that everyone was doing just then. To prepare the egg, we took a cup and laid plastic wrap over it. Then we took truffle oil and rubbed it on the bottom of the plastic just before cracking the egg into the cup. We would then wrap the egg and tie it with another piece of plastic wrap so that it was its own little package of stink. We then poached it for exactly six minutes in simmering water so it came out looking like a little purse. Vile, and also kind of genius.

I was responsible for the truffled egg dish, as well as two pastas, a handful of veg sides like lemon- and butter-glazed wax beans, brussels sprouts (a massive pain, since I had to spend nearly two hours of every day's prep time taking the individual leaves off), sardines with foam, and a pain-in-the-ass sweet potato dauphine. It was a lot going on for one station, especially since the egg dish was far and away the most popular, and it was stressful work, keeping track of six different eggs that were dropped in the same water at different times.

So, even though I picked up some new technique by proximity, the day-to-day at the Smith was boring as hell, I was under a bitchy chef with a lot to prove, and again, I was feeling restless. He seemed to take a sick joy in sending back my dishes, claiming they needed more or less salt. I was more or less his punching bag. Not only was I handling a deep-fryer, the egg-poaching liquid, numerous foams at different temperatures, and all the pastas, but I was also in charge of all the accoutrements for the other cooks' stations. There was nothing overtly wrong with the job—in fact, I got along well with the staff, but I still harbored disdain for a man channeling Napoleon and who seemed overly enthusiastic about the hype of our industry. But when I was done, I was done. One night, the kitchen was buzzing because Rocco DiSpirito was coming to dinner. The chef was excited, looking over all of our shoulders, and I suddenly felt myself completely lose hope in the people cooking the food. For the first and only time in my career, I walked out in the middle of prep service.

It was early fall when I left Smith's, and the snow was on its way. Chloe was now working at La Sirène, the French bistro below our apartment, and had picked up some secretary work on the side, so we weren't desperate. But I hated depending on her for money. Plus, shit never goes well when I'm not working. I needed a job, if for no other reason than to keep me out of trouble. The less time I had to think about doing drugs, the better. After I left Smith's, I spent the next several days walking the streets of downtown New York looking for restaurants to drop off my resume at.

The next place I landed turned out to be an important one for my career—Allen & Delancey. Like many of my other jobs, I happened upon it on a whim, just walking around the city and keeping my eyes open. I was on my way back home from a meeting in the East Village when I passed the building that housed the Lower East Side restaurant located, unsurprisingly, on the corner of Allen and Delancey streets. I walked in right before service and asked for the chef. I told the bartender that I was looking for a job as a cook and had a resume on hand that I could give them to look at right then. I guess sometimes having a pair of balls and nothing to lose comes in handy. The bartender disappeared and came back with a tall, redheaded man named Brian, who turned out to be the sous chef. He took a quick glance at my resume, asked me a few questions, and told me to return the next day for a stage. I had a good feeling that I was in.

After a bunch of shitty, no-name restaurant jobs, this felt like the first exciting opportunity in a long time. Allen & Delancey had a Michelin star It had two *New York Times* dining section stars. Standing in the kitchen, waiting for Brian to return, I let a little wave of excitement rush over me. I'd been dicking around in New York for too long, when this was the kind of restaurant I wanted to be at. This was why I'd moved to New York.

But along with all that prestige came another realization. Thanks in part to the leap of faith by Nora in DC, I'd been in sous or executive chef positions now since Savannah, which, in all honesty, was probably before I'd been ready for it. I knew I needed to clear my head a bit, get my shit together, and just cook for a while on the line. This seemed like the perfect opportunity. And, for a while at least, I did just that.

True to its reputation, Allen & Delancey had some truly talented cooks—certainly some of the best that I'd worked with until that point—and it's interesting to look back and see where they've ended up. The redheaded sous, Brian Leth, is now the chef de cuisine at Vinegar Hill House in Brooklyn. The pastry chef, Tiffany MacIsaac, now works with four or five different restaurants, including Birch & Barley and Vermilion.

They weren't fucking around at Allen & Delancey either. Before I arrived, the chef was a dude named Neil Ferguson, who had worked for Gordon Ramsay at The London, until he was fired after receiving only two *New York Times* stars. He then left Allen & Delancey after a dispute with the owners, which left just his two sous chefs in charge—Laura and Brian.

I mostly worked under Brian, as the tournant, and was responsible for three out of five stations.

The kitchen at Allen & Delancey was strangely shaped and separated into divisions, like a railroad car, which was like nothing I'd ever seen before. I mostly worked the entremetier station, which, by definition, means everything in the kitchen that doesn't have to do with meat and fish. At Allen & Delancey, it meant that I was responsible for every entrée's garnish, as well as my own risotto course. And that was no joke—every entrée had at least three or four extra components, and coordinating them was like running the air traffic control booth at JFK. Everything had a different veg, starch, puree, sauce. You name it and I had to plate it. Plus, in addition to doing all of that, or "picking up" the various elements during service, I was responsible for prepping them as well, and for prepping the rest of the cooks' mise en place (staple ingredients like fine herbs, shallot brunoise, beurre monté, etc.). In other words, I was pretty much everyone's little bitch.

I worked next to the pastry department on one side, which was pretty cool to watch, since I hadn't spent much time around pastry chefs at that point. There were three of them, maybe, working under MacIsaac, and they mostly kept to themselves and churned out some pretty awesome dishes. It was one of the first places I had worked where I could turn my head and see the Taylor Ice Cream Machine churning out delicious sweetened creams, and mini baguettes being sprayed with water for bread service.

But if it was peaceful in pastryland, the meat and fish station was on the other side of me, and that was fucking trouble.

The chef de partie of that station was named Matthew, and I couldn't stand him. He always had something to say, and not about food, either. He wanted to buddy-buddy up with everyone and took more smoke breaks during prep than an Indian chief preparing for a ritual. He always had a shit-eating grin on his face, and never cared about the collective work of the kitchen, putting his own ego before everything else. No one would correct him, though. Well, no one other than me. As any cook knows, if you're constantly in the shits, so much that you come in, daily, three hours before you're scheduled, and the buffoon next to you is taking smoke breaks while his sauce is over-reducing, you begin to build an unwavering hatred for your colleague. Looking back on the situation now, I just laugh—I mean, his claim to fame was that he was a personal chef. I can't help but see the similarities between what Carlos had felt for me at Nora and what I had felt for Matthew. I guess it really does all come full circle sometimes.

In many ways, my time at Allen & Delancey did exactly what I'd hoped it would do. For the most part, I kept my head down and cooked my ass off, and in doing that, it refined my competence as a cook. It helped me learn organizational skills, some new techniques, and, maybe most important, it helped me learn how to deal with personalities I didn't necessarily identify with or get along with.

On a day-to-day basis, though, it felt like all I did was make risotto. A lot of risotto. I made risotto until I swear to God my forearm was popping out of my chef's jacket like Popeye after a spinach binge. It seemed like I spent the majority of our six-hour service whipping sage and squash puree into the grains of Arborio, one giant stroke after another. Every plate had a puree, of course, so I spent a lot of time perfecting purees without the use of xanthan gum, which is often used as a crutch by many modern chefs to make up for errors in the production of the purees. My favorite was a parsley puree that we would use to color cauliflower florets for a bone marrow, pancetta-parmesan–crusted halibut and black trumpet mushroom course. I remember tasting the puree over and over again, to get the perfect balance between salinity, sweetness, and chlorophyll.

Between the risottos and purees, I also spent a lot more time on sauce work than I ever had before, got the opportunity to butcher meat, and worked with some new ingredients. It was everything I was looking for in that kind of job—prestigious restaurant, high-achieving chefs, new product, and the chance to work on my skills set. I stayed there through fall and early winter and left only when they decided to finally replace Ferguson with a new chef just after New Year's Eve. I didn't take issue with the new chef, and there wasn't any reason I needed to leave. But I had a particularly good connection with Brian, and when they hired the new chef, my loyalty to the restaurant ended. Plus, the usual restlessness was kicking in and I was ready for a new adventure.

If only I'd known what kind of adventure lay ahead.

∾

At that point in my life, I must say, it's a miracle that I hadn't yet gotten in any kind of legal trouble. I was twenty-three then, and it felt like I'd done enough drugs in the last four years to fuel the economy of a small South American country, but I hadn't so much as been arrested for drug possession or minor theft. My only run-in with the law was a traffic offense, from driving without a license in Florida years before. But that was all about to change in a major way.

As winter made its way into spring the year I left Allen & Delancey, I was so fucked up on coke that I can hardly tell you what I was doing day to day. I got hired as a sous chef in a little bistro in the West Village, and I'm being honest when I say that the time period was such a blur that I can't even remember the name of the restaurant or the chef who hired me.

None of that matters, though. The only thing that did matter from the job was that I befriended one of the cooks, and he soon became the solution to a familiar problem that was rearing its ugly head again. Six months after I'd moved back in with Chloe, the situation had become unbearable. I needed to get out of there, and quickly. With the cash I was making at the restaurant, I had a little to spare on rent, and the cook I'd befriended had space in what turned out to be a pretty swanky apartment above the Strand Book Store near Union Square. He also was about to leave on a monthlong vacation to Los Angeles, where he was from, so for the first month, I'd have the place all to myself.

I knew my drug problem was getting out of hand again— apart from a month here or there, I'd really never sprung back from my binges during Genevieve's pregnancy, and by this point, it was a fucking disaster. The meetings weren't cutting it, and I couldn't make myself go, so I knew it was only a matter of time before I checked myself into an actual rehab facility. But before I did that, I had another problem: I'd managed to rack up quite a debt to my drug dealers. I knew I needed to take care of it, and fast.

I moved into the new apartment near Union Square and spent that first month scraping together as much as I could to pay back the dealers. I managed to do so, and I was psyched—I could pay off my debts, order a couple of grams, and have one last binge before I packed up and finally got clean once and for all, or so my addict brain justified. Near the end of my friend's vacation, I called up the delivery service with enough money to do all that, and they agreed to come to the apartment to meet me. The drug dealers, however, had a different idea of how this would go down.

I'm not proud of what happened next. In fact, every time I think of it, I'm clouded with shame and regret. But, without sugarcoating it or trying to make myself feel like a victim, I'll tell it straight. The Dominican cocaine delivery service showed up at the apartment, and immediately after I opened the door, they burrowed past me and started ransacking the place. Within minutes, they cleared the unknowing, innocent cook's apartment of everything of value, while I stood by and nervously watched. I couldn't do anything, and we both knew it. There was no way I could stop them alone, especially if I didn't want to get killed. And I obviously couldn't call the cops. The only thing I could do was get the fuck out of there.

As soon as they left, I ran. And for the next six months, I was basically a fugitive. I shacked up on the Upper East Side with a girl I used to do coke with, and completely fell out of contact with anyone I had known. It was a dark time. All the resolve that I'd had about getting clean vanished on that night, and I was higher than I'd ever been in my life, wanting to escape what had just happened. I couldn't believe I'd been so stupid, that I'd gotten myself in such a mess, and that I'd fucked over a friend in the process.

But this could only last so long. I knew the NYPD was looking for me, and there was no way in hell I was planning on turning myself in. Chloe had called to warn me that the detective handling the case had left his card under her door. But I couldn't hide on the Upper East Side forever. Besides, I figured, it was the NYPD. At that point the charges were almost six months old, and it's not like it was a murder or anything. If the police didn't have better things to worry about than my fairly minor crime, I figured something was fucked up.

So I did what I needed to do. I got a job. I wasn't looking for anything fancy, and took the first thing that came along— a gig at a little place called City Girl Café on Thompson Street in SoHo. But even though there are nine fucking million people in New York City, I should have remembered how small it really can be. It was literally my first day of work when a customer recognized me, knew the situation, and turned me in. I had barely been slinging lattes for two hours when I was arrested for grand larceny.

A lot of things are foggy about that period, but I remember the arrest as clearly as if it had happened yesterday, and I suspect it's something I'll never forget, no matter how much I've pickled my brain since then. I was behind the counter, making coffees, when two burly detectives walked up to the counter and asked my name. They'd recognized me immediately from my tattoos, which, I suppose, is a good lesson for all fugitives—if you have a knife and fork on your throat, and other identifying marks, it can be a bit hard to hide.

Within minutes, I was in handcuffs. I never saw a badge, and I'd be lying if I said I was 100 percent sure they were even cops. I had been involved with some serious criminals, and it occurred to me that this might be an elaborate plot by the drug dealers to get me somewhere no one could see in order to "deal" with me. Either way, I was scared shitless.

But it all became clear within the next hour. They took me to the 1st Precinct, off Varick Street in Tribeca, made me sign a document with my Miranda rights, and started to level with me.

"This is an open-and-shut case, Mr. Baltzley," said one detective. "We have an eyewitness who said you were there. You don't look like a criminal. I know criminals; you aren't one. If you talk to us, we may be able to help you."

I've always hated the idea of snitching—it was just something that, growing up in my part of Jacksonville, we didn't do. But I've never had a problem with accepting responsibility and owning up when I was a part of something.

Without hesitating, I told the detective, "I was there. I didn't do it or plan it, but I did not do anything to stop it."

He let me smoke my entire pack of cigarettes in the interrogation room and then led me out of the room and put me back in the car. We were on our way to the Manhattan Detention Complex, located in Lower Manhattan and known to everyone in the city as The Tombs. The name is ominous for a reason, and I was nervous as hell. I had never been to jail before, and jail in New York City sounded fucking horrifying. With every block we passed, my stomach churned more and more and my palms started to sweat. I didn't know how I'd gotten myself into this, and all I wanted was to get out in one piece.

The Tombs, I'd quickly come to learn, are basically the equivalent of purgatory. It's the waiting room, more or less, to the arraignment at the courthouse. If you get arrested or even accused of something, it is mandatory that you go to The Tombs and wait to be seen by a judge, which could happen any time from twelve hours to three days, depending on when you get there.

And they weren't kidding with the name, either. This place looked like something out of fucking *Batman*. It's in a gigantic building near Chinatown, and you enter through a garage door into a long, half-lit hallway with a yellow line down the center. I walked on one side, and the detective dropping me off walked on the other. After a series of turns, bends, and flickering fluorescent lights, I began to think this was some kind of joke. We finally got to a checkpoint, where I was checked in by a nurse, then walked what seemed like another mile down a hallway. I had my mug shots taken, and walked for what seemed yet another mile. I was handed a sandwich and a box of cereal, then walked another very long distance into the actual cell. It was extremely disorienting to change directions so many times, which I'm sure was on purpose, to make it impossible to escape. By the time I reached my cell, I didn't know what the fuck was going on.

Cells are separated according to the severity of charges,

but all of them are damp, cold, and soaked in piss. I'd guess there were about thirty people in mine, which was basically an eighteen-by-eighteen-foot concrete hole-in-the-wall, with one toilet in the middle and a bench around the perimeter that you definitely wanted to get a seat on. It was clear that the majority of my fellow tenants for the night were also drug addicts.

Before he dropped me off, the detective said one thing that stuck in my head: "Just watch out for the people that are sleeping. The ones that can sleep in there are the ones that should be in there." He was right. I ended up being in for about eighteen hours, and wouldn't have been able to sleep a wink even if it meant that all charges against me would be dropped.

After a fair amount of sizing one another up, I took my seat and waited. To my right was a baby-faced kid who looked so young I couldn't believe he could possibly be charged as an adult. He was caught with twenty vials of "hard," meaning crack, and some pot for his own use—with that kind of stash, I imagine he spent the next three years upstate. There was a homeless man lying on the piss-stained concrete floor below me, and every once in a while, he would go into convulsions, similar to a seizure, from crack withdrawal. I flinched every time he seized up again, hoping like hell that he wasn't going to die at my feet. I remember a man so dope sick that he spent most of the night screaming from atop the stainless steel toilet bowl (with no lid) that he couldn't take a proper shit.

The only person I could really talk to was the man to my left, a hardened drug dealer from Bushwick who had gotten caught with a handgun in Chinatown earlier that morning. He took one look at me and shook his head.

"You don't look like you should be in here, cuz," he said.

And he was right. This wasn't the place for me—every fiber in my being knew that. I hadn't wanted my friend's apartment to be robbed. I hadn't meant for it to happen. Even though I knew I was at the scene of the crime. Even though I knew I could've called the cops anytime in the past six months and at least cleared that small pocket of my conscience. I knew, at heart, that I wasn't really a criminal. I had let something happen, but I still had a conscience. And that felt like enough.

The bald, muscular black man's mouth opened up under a bristly mustache. "What they got you for?"

"Grand larceny," I replied.

"First time?"

"Yeah." I nodded back.

"You do it?"

"Kind of," I said. "It's complicated."

He smiled at me.

"It always is, cousin. It always is."

At around five A.M., we were shuffled to a new cell, closer to the courthouse. The sun wasn't up yet, but there were new officers. I knew the arraignment couldn't be much further away, which gave me hope. Anything to make this process end. But time seemed to inch along. And, if possible, this cell was somehow even worse than the last one. There were no seats, except on the opposite side of bar-covered windows peering into the free world. And it was fucking freezing. Every person in the cell immediately turned into turtles, quickly re-tracting their limbs into their white tees. One dude just lay facedown on the floor and went back to sleep. I remembered what the detective had told me. That's the one to look out for.

After what felt like four hours but was probably more like twenty minutes, public defenders began to come to the win-dows and call out, one after the other, inmates' names. Fi-nally, I heard mine: "Brandon Ba . . . ltz . . . ley. Brandon Baltzley!"

It was a young woman's voice, and she sounded like she had woken up ten minutes before stepping foot in the court-house. I went up to the window and was surprised by how attractive she was. Laura had long blond hair and was wear-ing a pantsuit, neither of which I would consider myself a fan of, but still . . . she was a cute girl. I immediately felt at ease, and then felt bad for her when I thought about the more "long-term" clients she dealt with. The whole process was quick. She asked if I did it, genuinely listened to my explanation, and just told me to be quiet, respond when spoken to, and let her deal with it. Then she was done with me, and on to the next.

A few hours later, we were gathered once again and led through a hallway into the courthouse. After spending the night in the dank tombs, the light streaming in through the windows, combined with the deep fluorescent lights, was prac-tically blinding. People were buzzing around everywhere—civilians, lawyers, officers, and inmates—and all bathed in this ridiculous light. I had to blink several times just to let my eyes adjust to all the light. If I hadn't known better, I could have sworn I was on acid.

There was also something obviously symbolic about the light. It had been a night full of darkness—but it was so much more than just that night. I'd spent the last six months hiding, scared of this very moment, of getting caught and having to own up to what I'd done. And I'd spent the last year letting myself get so out of control that I was driven to the night that led to these charges. In some ways, it felt like I'd been in The Tombs for a whole lot longer than eighteen hours. And being there that morning, really seeing that blinding light, was like someone shaking me, like someone saying, "Hey, Brandon. It's time to wake up."

After waiting my turn, I was called to the stand. The prosecutor wanted to set bail at five thousand dollars and charge me with a class D felony. But Laura argued the case well, making the case that I was a first-time offender with nothing more than a drug problem. Clearly, I hadn't intended for this to happen. I was let go on my own recognizance and was summoned back a month later.

When I appeared in court again, the class D felony lessened, and it lessened the longer I stayed out of trouble and paid back the worth of the stolen merchandise to my former roommate. I ended up with nothing more than an order of protection against the person who was stolen from and a criminal mischief charge which, I was reminded numerous times, is a ticketed violation and not a crime. I guess this is what happens when you're a young white male. I'd hate to hear what happened to the rest of my one-night cellmates.

I'd love to say that, after my arrest, I was ready to change my life right away. But I still had a long road ahead of me. It would take going to a rehab program in Staten Island and countless more meetings at Narcotics Anonymous to finally figure out a new direction. A path that would end up leading me to a Michelin three-star restaurant in Chicago and a very public fall from grace. It wasn't until I was able to get another three months clean and took a job at an Irish pub in the West Village that I met the person who would make all that possible. And, to this day, I wonder if my lives would have run out had I not been introduced to the daytime server at Mr. Dennehy's. It's funny how life works sometimes. But when I look back on it, it's easy to see how a shitty Irish pub that no one would ever look at twice had put me on my path to Alinea.

CHAPTER SIX

It was early in the winter after my arrest that I finally hit what I'd call rock bottom. I'd been living in New York for almost three years at that point, flitting between jobs like a moth with a short attention span. Part of the job changes were the industry, of course. It's a transient world, and New York is a particularly transient place. And some of the moves weren't my fault. I worked at Bouley Upstairs for a month, for example, and they didn't pay me a dime. After a while, I quit asking for my money and just stopped showing up.

But just as many moves had everything to do with me and, even more specifically, with my addiction. At that point, I'd been using steadily for five or six years, and even though I'd tried to get clean tons of times, nothing seemed to stick. I'd check myself into rehab, stay for twenty-four hours, bail, and go right back to using. It was all so easy in New York. You didn't even have to go out on the streets to score. Just call a number, and they'd deliver to your door, like a pizza.

The summer after I was arrested, I did manage, for the first time, to finally complete a program—thirty days of hell in some state-run rehab on Staten Island with cold fish sticks and these bored counselors who so clearly didn't give a fuck. I had checked myself into the program, but almost everyone else there was mandated by the state, and I didn't find the support system I needed to succeed. I knew I was teetering pretty damn close to the edge, so I stuck it out, and tried hard when I got out to stay with it.

One of the program's suggestions was to get what they called a "clean job," which basically meant anything to keep you busy and give you a paycheck without stressing you out too much. It didn't have to advance your career or stimulate you or any of that. It just had to pay the bills, and distract you, so you weren't trying to use. For me, that meant a "consulting chef" gig at Mr. Dennehy's, a tourist trap of an Irish pub in the West Village.

It was clear from the start that I didn't belong there, cranking out burgers and plates of fish-and-chips, after working at several Michelin-starred restaurants. And neither did one of the servers, a girl named Jacqueline who I started hanging out with. Jacqueline was a total contradiction. Despite her Jewish last name and the fact that she'd grown up on the Upper West Side, she was a blond, blue-eyed German. She didn't have the fine dining experience that I did, but she did have a degree from a prestigious college and, unlike everyone else who was working at Mr. Dennehy's, aspirations that extended far beyond the shepherd's pies she had to tote around every day.

At that point, my personal life was in a weird kind of purgatory. By the time I got the job at Dennehy's, I'd been broken up with Chloe for almost a year, but because we had a joint lease, we were still living together. She slept in the bed, and I slept on the couch. Needless to say, it was awkward as hell, especially when I was dating other girls, and she was probably dating other guys, but I wouldn't know since we never spoke. The situation couldn't hold much longer.

Jacqueline and I were just friends, but when she found out about my living situation, she offered to let me crash with her instead. We were just supposed to be roommates, and even though I thought of her as a friend then, I can see now that she probably always had feelings for me. And about three weeks after moving in together, we were sleeping together, too.

It was after I moved in with Jacqueline that everything started to really take a downhill plunge. Neither of us had belonged at Mr. Dennehy's, and so both of us left, but our paths couldn't have been more different. I took another "clean" job, at a coffee shop called Doma a few blocks away in the West Village. It wasn't bad, as far as shitty little filler jobs go. They paid me in cash, and the staff was cool— all, for some reason, hot Eastern European chicks, which was fine by me. I was the only one in the kitchen, and I could make sandwiches and salads in my sleep, so mostly I just plugged in my iPod and chilled out.

But while I was doing that, Jacqueline was hired as a host at Per Se.

I tried to be happy for her. I cared about her and I wanted what was best for her, and this was an incredible opportunity that she couldn't pass up. But in reality, I was so fucking jealous

I couldn't see straight, and right from the beginning, it ate at me like a parasite. She didn't have anything close to the restaurant experience I had, but all of a sudden, she was at the absolute pinnacle of American fine dining, and I was making bowls of lentil soup for yuppies on laptops. It was infuriating, almost suffocating, and no matter how hard I tried, I couldn't shake it.

So I responded in the only way I knew how—by relapsing. I'd been clean for a few months after finishing the rehab program on Staten Island, but when Jacqueline was hired at Per Se, I let it all go. And I don't just mean a beer here and there. My fall was immediate, hard, and so desperate, it scared the shit out of me. I was drunk all the time, and then I was doing coke, and then, for the first time since I'd sworn off it nearly four years earlier in DC, I got back into crack.

Doma worked like a clean job was supposed to, in one sense. I wasn't stressed out at all. But instead of keeping me off drugs, it left plenty of time and energy for me to get obliterated every day and still muddle through my job without much of a problem. In the middle of almost every service, I'd take a break, or several, and head downstairs to the basement, where we did our prep work, to smoke a pipe. Usually after work, I was ready for more, so I'd catch an L train out to Bushwick to hang with an addict friend named Carmen, a little hipster girl with neon pink spandex and yellow sunglasses who was always down to party. I didn't even like her, really, but she was always ready to get fucked up, and at that point, that was all that mattered to me. Sometimes I made it home to Jacqueline's afterward. Sometimes I didn't.

I think I was using so much not only because I wasn't

happy with where I was then, but because I'd convinced my-self that my career was over forever. I knew I was talented, that cooking was something I was naturally good at. And I'd risen so high so quickly that my options had at times almost felt limitless. I understood on some level that I had what it would take to succeed, to really succeed, to Per Se–level suc-ceed, in the culinary world. But now that I'd let myself get so far from that world, and I had to watch Jacqueline come home from it every night, I was afraid it was too late. That I'd thrown it all away for good.

The more I thought about it, the deeper I dug my own hole. No part of me could fathom climbing out of this and picking up where I had left off, so it didn't matter anymore how low I sank. I was using more than I ever had before, go-ing on manic binges where I plowed through thousands of dollars of coke in a week, and then wading through the rest of life in a fog.

And then, something in me broke.

I wanted out, and at that point, I only knew one way that was guaranteed to do it. At the beginning of November, I stole four hundred dollars from Jacqueline's purse when she was out, and left the apartment. I used maybe eighty of it on a little room at the Bowery Hotel and spent the rest on crack, then went to the hotel by myself, checked in, and did all of it—probably four full grams—in five minutes, hoping to God that I wouldn't have to wake up and fight it—my addiction, my ru-ined potential, any of it—anymore. That it would just kill me.

I blacked out for a while, and when I came to, early in the morning, I had physically never felt worse in my life. The pain in my head was unbearable, rivaled only by the bile coming up the back of my throat and the tremors shaking my core. I was a seriously sorry sack of shit that morning.

But I didn't want to die anymore. I know it sounds like some sort of religious epiphany, or something you'd see on the back of a self-help book with a motivational speaker in a bad comb-over on the front cover. But it wasn't like that. I didn't see the light and hear someone telling me it wasn't my time to go yet. I couldn't, in that moment, see everything getting better if I just gave myself the chance of life again. All I can say is that when I woke up, the complete desperation, the feeling that death was the only way out of this absolute hell I was living, had gone. And I did know that I needed help, immediately.

I don't remember much about that morning, except that I made it out of the hotel, sick and shaking and out of my mind. I couldn't even get it together to hail a cab, couldn't trust my mouth to work and find the right words, so I just kept walking north. It felt like days, though it was probably closer to an hour, before I eventually ended up at the front door of Bellevue Hospital. I told them that I'd tried to overdose on crack, and they admitted me on the spot, and kept me there for two full weeks.

The days passed slowly and I began to snap out of it enough to realize that I probably didn't need to be in a mental hospital—not with people who talked to themselves and saw faces in the bathroom sinks and honestly believed they were the Incredible Hulk. The doctors diagnosed me as bipolar and pumped me full of Klonopin and Abilify and a bunch of other shit, but even through the haze of all the drugs, I couldn't figure out what the fuck I was doing there. I didn't have the perspective yet to see that I'd been so unhappy, so disappointed in myself that I'd let myself fall so far on purpose. I just thought I'd been high and stupid.

I will say one thing for spending time in a mental hospital—it gave me a lot of time to think. I was too drugged up to make much sense of anything or to have a clear idea of what had gone wrong in the last year that had led me to this point. But I thought about growing up, about my family, about women I'd loved, and places I'd been. And I thought about music. Over and over again, I heard the beating of drums, the one thing in my life that had, until the last few years, been as consistent as cooking.

I'd been playing the drums since I was a teenager. Like chopping corn for my mom's corn chowder, it was something productive that I could do with what felt like boundless energy. I played in the marching band at two different high schools, but what I really lived for was playing in punk and metal bands in my friends' garages. I was usually in three or four bands at a time, and had pretty much exhausted the Jacksonville scene by the time I left for Savannah when I was nineteen.

But what I really thought about, those two weeks in the mental hospital, was much bigger than a few years in my friends' basements as a teenager. I thought about another path I could have taken, another one that I did end up taking for a few years. When I wasn't a cook at all but a musician for real, touring the country as the drummer for Kylesa.

I'd gotten the hookup for Kylesa through my ex-girlfriend, Lisa in Savannah, a woman I never thought I'd hear from again. Our breakup had been bad, and I was bitter when I left Savannah, first to return to Jacksonville, then for a short stint in St. Augustine, Florida, an old, beautiful city that felt to me a lot like Savannah. I was working there at a "fine dining" tourist trap and was bored as hell when Lisa called. She wasn't stupid—she knew I didn't want to hear from her—but she had an offer that I couldn't resist. I hadn't been that into metal at the time—punk and hardcore were more my scene—but Kylesa was getting big, and they needed a drummer. I didn't have anything else going on, so I told her to pass along my number.

I talked to the bassist and we hit it off, so he asked me to learn a few songs off their album over the next few days and then come up to Savannah to audition for them. That sounded fine in theory, except for one big problem—I didn't have a drum set. But, if nothing else, I've always been good at improvising. I found a bunch of phone books, set them up like a drum set, grabbed a pair of Vic Firths, and got to work.

Over the next five days, I learned the entire Kylesa album on those phone books, and then I was ready to roll. I caught a ride back up to Savannah, met up with the band, and told them I had to borrow some drums. The looks on their faces when I told them how I'd learned all their songs was priceless, and to this day I wonder whether that's what pushed me over the edge to get the job. Either way, I passed the audition with flying colors. And then the second, less formal audition—they were hard drinkers and wanted to make sure I could keep up. Needless to say, I did.

Kylesa was getting ready to go on tour, and I had exactly a month and a half to learn all of their songs before we left, which meant pretty much devoting my entire life to the band. I moved into their house—or close to it. I slept on a futon mattress on the back porch, which was covered in palmetto bugs and smelled like turpentine. Not yet the glamorous musician lifestyle I'd envisioned. Still, none of us had to have day jobs— Kylesa brought in enough money to keep us fed and drunk, and that was all we cared about.

Then we left on tour, and suddenly we were playing shows bigger than I'd ever imagined. The high of playing crowds like that is almost indescribable—the noise, the lights, the sheer intensity of so many people there to listen to us. Sitting in the eerie quiet of my hospital room in Bellevue so many years later, I could sometimes hear the echo of shows in my ears, and for hours I would be lost in it, remembering countless clubs in countless cities across the country.

But touring with a band like that was also taxing in a way I never would have imagined. Physically, I was exhausted. That kind of music takes serious showmanship, and as the drummer, I was on the entire time. I mean, I beat the living shit out of my drums, to the point at which I came to expect vomiting and muscle spasms every single damn day. Even making it through a forty-five-minute set became hard. I would throw my back and neck out so violently that all I could do after a show was sit and drink. I would sleep in the tour van every day all the way to our next destination, where I would set up my drums, drink a few beers, and do it all over again.

The lifestyle was also pretty insane—we were on the road for nine months of the year, returning to Savannah only for about a month at a time. We all had significant others and friends and family, and keeping up those relationships began to feel impossible. Plus, we were surviving on fifty dollars per diem. We mostly drank for free, and spent some money on weed and cigarettes, leaving us a few pennies for ramen noodles, cans of black beans, and scrambled eggs.

I stayed with Kylesa for a year and a half, and in many ways, it was the best time of my life. We recorded a full-length album, which was released by Prosthetic Records. Ultimately, it was something that screwed me over, because I didn't sign a contract until after the album was released. But knowing that it's out there, a tangible product of this time I had and the music we created, is still something. I got to travel, to see the country, to meet some of the best people I know even to this day. I smoked weed and watched the sun rise over the Pacific Ocean. I played to a sold-out crowd at New York's Bowery Ballroom, and Emo's in Austin, and the Triple Rock in Minneapolis. I went out of the country for the first time—to Canada and Mexico, and I'm not just talking about Tijuana bullshit. It was a crazy time, but it was fun as hell, too.

But, of course, being on the road all the time is one of the hardest fucking things any group of people can do. Tension inevitably started to build within the band. There was already a dark cloud over things when I joined—the previous bassist had died of an epileptic seizure, and I guess the chemistry was never exactly right with the new group. After about a year, I came to hate one of the band members so much that I started to catch rides with other bands on the way to the next city.

Finally, though, something happened that broke me. Neil, a close friend from Jacksonville, committed suicide, and I didn't learn about it until a week later. I was devastated. I was ruined. My entire world felt like it was turned upside down. And just when I needed my bandmates to be my friends, to care about me and support me as I was reeling from such a tragedy, it seemed they were anything but. I didn't feel I had anything to turn to but drugs to ease the pain, and I found myself doing more and more coke, hoping it would numb the fact that Neil was gone. And the more coke I did, the more things went badly with my bandmates until, finally, I felt I had no choice but to leave.

I thought a lot about that time while I was in the hospital, and especially about Neil. It was the first time I really started to understand how he must have been feeling when he killed himself, how much pain he must have been in. At the time, we were just dumb kids. I didn't have a fucking care in the world. But sitting there in Bellevue, feeling like I had nothing, I really got it for the first time. I wished that Neil hadn't been successful, either. I wished that he was sitting there with me, with another chance in his pocket, too. And, in honor of him, through the haze of all the shit they had me on, I knew I'd try to do better for both of us.

Amazingly enough, Jacqueline stayed with me through the whole thing. She was pissed at first, and tried to get out of the relationship. But I was as honest with her as possible, and eventually she came around. She visited me every day in the hospital, bringing me sandwiches and reminding me that there was normal life outside those walls. That there were people who didn't think they were comic book characters. And even, that as much as I'd tried to shut it out and deny it, that there were things and people waiting for me on the other side.

Bellevue released me just before Thanksgiving, and suddenly there was nothing I wanted to do more than to go home to Jacksonville to see my family for the holiday. I needed to get out of New York for a little while, to think things through, to see if I was really meant to be there. And I wanted to see my mom.

Thanksgiving came and went, but I couldn't make myself go back to New York. So I just put it off and put it off, until eventually I'd been hanging out in Jacksonville for the entire month of December. I'd almost convinced myself that maybe I ought to stay for good—that I just hadn't been cut out for New York—and I started looking for work in Florida. But the restaurant scene there was as dry as a fucking desert. All I could do was day labor—power washing ritzy private schools out in the suburbs, holding stop signs for construction sites, shit like that. I'd work a ten-hour day and come home with a thirty-five-dollar paycheck. Not really worth sticking around for. And Jacksonville wasn't helping me get clean, either, even when that whole episode in New York should've been enough to scare me straight forever. It's never been easy for me to stay sober in Jacksonville, which is where I started drinking and using in the first place. My mom quit coke a while ago, but she's never given up drinking, so there was lots of that still going on at home. And every once in a while, even despite everything, I'd disappear at night and go get high with my friends.

So if Jacksonville wasn't the answer, I finally resigned myself to giving New York another chance. Instead of flying, I boarded an all-night Amtrak train north from Florida on New Year's Eve, and as the ball dropped in Times Square that year, ushering in 2010, I was in the club car, drinking Bud Light and playing poker with two fifty-year-old gay guys from Cleveland.

I arrived in New York early in the morning and headed back to Jacqueline's apartment on the Upper West Side, and for a little while, it seemed as if not all that much had changed. I'd get up, look for work, get bored and frustrated when I couldn't find anything, and start drinking. Even doing coke every once in a while. On top of that, I was already getting hooked on the Klonopin they'd put me on at Bellevue. In just those couple of weeks back in New York, I could feel myself slipping back into the same routine that had nearly killed me that fall.

I wanted to catch myself before I fell even further, and didn't want to add a new addiction to my already impressive arsenal, so I decided in the middle of January to get rid of the Klonopin before it also started getting bad, and checked myself into a three-day detox. I can't say it was a particularly major decision to go, and looking back, I don't even count it toward my sobriety. It felt like I had a full army to fight, and I was just killing off a soldier or two on the front line, before they got too close.

But it was a step, and clearly something did change. When I woke up in Jacqueline's apartment on my first day out of the detox, my head was clearer than I could remember it being in ages.

It was January 22, 2010, a Friday, early morning, and the day before my twenty-fifth birthday.

I got out of bed, careful not to wake Jacqueline, who had worked late the night before, and wandered over to the window. It had been a brutal winter so far, and the glass was already fogged over, like someone had sprayed it with a can of fake snow. I rubbed away the dew and looked down.

On the street, people were starting to leave for work, headed for the subways in droves, wearing suits and button-up shirts, and carrying their briefcases. I used to think they were all suckers, heading off to desks to stare at computers all day without actually doing anything. But that morning, something about it struck me as oddly comforting, even appealing. They were doing something steady at least.

Something they'd keep doing day after day. Making money, keeping a roof over their heads. All that shit that had always seemed sort of like a secondary concern for me.

I rubbed my eyes, stretched, and pressed my nose against the glass, watching them walk to the subway. Would I ever be like that? Putting on a suit and going to work, at the same place, every day? I couldn't see it. But I couldn't see this, either, hopping from job to job, crashing with a friend or a girl or whoever I could. Making money just to make money, without really caring about what I was doing. Would this be where I was when I was thirty? When I was forty?

Jacqueline came up behind me in her pajamas, hand curled around a coffee cup, and put her arm around my waist.

"Happy almost birthday," she said, kissing my shoulder.

I stayed at the window.

"Thanks."

"So, the big two-five. Are you ready for it?"

I looked at her, then back out the window, and shrugged.

"Hard to say." I yawned. "I guess I better be."

"Well, how about this to ease you into it . . ." she said. "I got tomorrow night off, and we have eight o'clock reservations for the tasting menu at wd~50."

My ears perked up. Wylie Dufresne was like the David Copperfield of cooking, and wd~50 was his flagship. I'd been once before, and remembered being intrigued by what he was doing, though nothing in particular had stood out. But I hadn't had his tasting menu, which I'd heard was like a full-on, no-holds-barred culinary magic show.

I admit that, up until this point, I hadn't given much serious thought to molecular gastronomy, and when I had, I was skeptical. It had been growing in popularity over the last dec ade and had recently skyrocketed, in part due to shows like *Top Chef* and *Top Chef Masters*, where Wylie Dufresne had been a contestant.

Thanks to them, it seemed like everyone—even people who didn't know how to grill a simple piece of meat or make a demi-glace—all of a sudden wanted to get into liquid nitrogen and shit like that.

I'm no food snob, and I know firsthand that cooking goes far beyond a diploma from Le Cordon Bleu. I never went to culinary school, so I've always been a proponent of just experimenting like hell until you find something in the kitchen that works. But I did learn from executive chefs who focused on simple flavors done well, and at that time, it was the only cooking philosophy I had.

As far as I was concerned, food was food. If you got the right ingredients, paired them into the right flavor profiles, and used the right technique, then it would be good. Pretty simple equation, if you asked me. And anyone who needed a goddamn science lab in their kitchen was probably overcompensating for something else. I was curious to see what Wylie Dufresne was doing back there, but it was going to take a lot for him to impress me.

And the weird thing is, he did it with a dish I didn't even particularly like. Or, to put it more strongly, was one of the most viscerally disgusting things I've ever eaten. A dish that, when I think about it today, nearly two years later (and I do think about it, all the time, actually), literally makes me start to gag a little bit. But it was also the dish that changed, fundamentally, who I am as a chef.

It was listed as a scrambled egg ravioli with charred avocado. I wasn't sure what to expect—maybe a play on carbonara, or an avocado filling with a coddled egg sauce? But what arrived was completely baffling. A tube of some sort of avocado puree charred dark with a blowtorch, a piece of raw kampachi, and a freestanding, bright yellow cube. Just sitting on the plate like a plexiglass sculpture.

I turned the plate to look from a different angle, trying to figure out what was going on with the ravioli. Was it a wonton wrapper dipped in egg? A light egg pasta? But how could it be standing like this? I poked at it with the side of my fork, and it jiggled slightly, like an egg would. And then I took a bite, and my mind was blown. The entire thing was made entirely of scrambled egg. The filling, the walls of the "pasta." Everything. I called over the waiter, and he confirmed. The filling was egg scrambled with cream cheese and gelatin, and then frozen into cubes.

Each cube was then dipped in more egg yolk that had been mixed with xanthan gum, and then skewered and boiled. As the outer layer cooked, it formed a ravioli-like cube, the skewer slipped out, and the inner layer defrosted into a soft filling. It was rich, and creamy, almost overwhelmingly so, and the melding of two kinds of eggy textures felt off-putting to me. My stomach lurched a little as it settled in. But in other ways, it was incredible.

Suddenly, I was six years old again, standing on a step stool after school in our kitchen in Jacksonville, with a carton of eggs in one hand, and the other hand plunged deep into my mother's spice cabinet. I'd been making scrambled eggs since I could walk. Since they were so cheap and there wasn't that much a little kid could do to fuck them up, my mom pretty much gave me free rein over them, which meant that they were the first food I remember experimenting with. I'd go through the entire dozen in one sitting, in the afternoons when my mom wasn't home, trying them with one thing and then another, until I found combinations I liked.

And literally in one bite, wd~50 had completely changed

the way I thought about scrambled eggs. About how they could taste and what they could be. I might not have liked the dish, but it opened up an entire planet of things that, with the right flavor combinations, could be amazing.

We meandered through the rest of the tasting menu, which was just as full of tricks and complicated technique as I had expected. I loved some of them, like the cold fried chicken—fried and then cooled to near freezing temperature and served with a buttermilk ricotta—and the incredible array of pastries that included black yuzu with sesame, mangoes, and popcorn, and a soft chocolate cake packet filled with beets and ricotta ice cream. But I couldn't stop thinking about that fucking scrambled egg.

Maybe, if that scrambled egg was possible, there was a way to think conceptually about food, to really tell a story on a plate, without sacrificing the simple flavor profiles that were so fundamental to my cooking. Maybe molecular gastronomy didn't have to be all about tricks for the sake of tricks. Maybe there was a way to actually use it to make people think about their food in different ways. To combine things that I knew worked already, but in a way no one had done before. Maybe food could, like the scrambled egg ravioli had just done for me, be comforting and nostalgic, while still being something totally brand-new.

We left the restaurant close to midnight and headed west into the frigid January night, toward the subway. It was windy, and the cold gusts whipped around the buildings on Allen Street, blowing into our faces. But to me, it felt invigorating. I hadn't had this much energy in months, maybe even years. It was like being high, only my head was clear and my heartbeat steady, and there wouldn't be any crash at the end of it.

I knew in that moment that my career wasn't over. That I hadn't even begun to cook the way I wanted to. There was a big fucking hurdle standing in the way of that. But I was just going to have to learn how to jump.

I put my arm around Jacqueline's shoulder as we walked, drew her close to me, and thanked her for the dinner. "It was the perfect way to spend my birthday."

Jacqueline looked at her watch.

"You've still got ten minutes left. Any final requests?"

I grinned.

"No final requests," I said. "But one thought."

"Oh, yeah?"

"Remember you asked me this morning how it felt to be twenty-five?"

"Sure."

"Well, I have an answer now," I said, and paused. "It feels like it's time to get clean."

She smiled, nodding perhaps a little too enthusiastically, though I guess she had the right.

"Great! So . . . back to rehab?"

"No," I answered, "I think I need to try doing this on my own."

"For real this time?"

I nodded. "Yeah. Cold turkey. I'm done with all of it."

"Good," she said, gripping me tighter, "because if you ever put me through this again, I will leave you so fast you won't have any idea what hit you."

"I promise. This time is for real."

I don't know how to explain it, but even though I'd tried and failed to get clean so many times before, I knew at that exact moment that I meant it. This time would be different.

The next morning, I woke up sweating and shaking with a fever. My head was heavy, my body was racked with chills, and I moved in a pathetic rotation between the bed, the couch, and the bathroom, where I lost everything I'd eaten the night before. I couldn't figure out what was wrong, and even now I don't know. It could have been a total coincidence—a stomach flu, or even, I guess, a freak case of food poisoning. It seems like it should've been the drugs, but I had just gotten out of the detox program, so it couldn't have been withdrawal, at least not in a physical sense. Even though I'm not one who usually buys into this kind of hokey shit, part of me can't help but believe that getting so sick that next morning was a sort of necessary last fight. Like I was forcing away all the ugliness, the demons that had had control of my body for so long.

I stayed like that for three days. And then, on the fourth, I got up and did two things. First, I got a temporary job filling in as a line cook at Salumeria Rosi, a casual spot on the Upper West Side, run in part by the Italian culinary legend Cesare Casella. It was the perfect kind of "clean" job for me, as opposed to Mr. Dennehy's. Easy, stress-free, with a little finger dipped into the fine dining world, and an understanding that it was temporary—just until I found something real. Second, I went to a meeting.

Even though I knew that Narcotics Anonymous could work, I'd already been to so many of their New York meetings and hadn't been successful that I thought it might help to go to Alcoholics Anonymous this time instead, at least to try something different. Maybe I'd relate to the program philosophy better, or vibe with the people better. Or maybe it would just be a new start. Anything was worth a try.

I was skeptical during my first meeting. Addiction is addiction, but since most of the people there hadn't done hard drugs, there were whole parts of my story that I felt they couldn't relate to. And more to the point, I didn't seem to have anything else in common with anyone there. They were older, for the most part, with white-collar jobs and families and shit like that. Not exactly my kind of people.

I felt discouraged at the end of the meeting—definitely not ready to give up on my decision to get clean, but also not convinced that AA was going to be the group to help get me there—when, just as I was leaving, this little squirrelly guy in a suit caught up to me and said he wanted to talk. His name was Bill, and he was older than me, probably by twenty years, and clearly rich, with an expensive suit and leather briefcase. He told me he was in digital marketing—he'd made a fortune making YouTube ads or something and had been clean for almost a decade.

We made small talk for a few more minutes, standing in the hallway of the church basement as everyone else shuffled out past us, but I couldn't quite figure out what he wanted with me—a twenty-five-year-old tattooed chef with three days' sobriety.

"Look, man," I started to say, "I really appreciate your help and all, and I'm really inspired by your sobriety, but—"

"I don't mean to be presumptuous," he interrupted, "but I think I might know someone who might change your mind about AA. My friend Chris. He's my age, sober for eleven years now, and we've been going to meetings together for years. I don't know. I just see a lot of him in you."

Bill handed me a slip of paper with a phone number scrawled on it.

"You might want to give him a call."

I thanked him and stuffed the paper in my wallet, with a pile of old receipts and a few crumpled dollar bills. I wasn't sure this guy knew what he was talking about, and I felt I was being set up on the AA equivalent of a blind date.

But when another meeting went by and I didn't find anyone I wanted to take on as my sponsor, I decided I didn't have anything to lose.

As it turned out, Bill was the best matchmaker in the city. To say that I had a lot in common with Chris Genoversa was a massive understatement. It was almost uncanny, and we hit it off right away. Chris isn't a Southerner—he's a straight-talking no-bullshit Brooklynite, born and raised in Sheeps-head Bay—but he has the same kind of fucked-up family dynamics I'd grown up with. Like me, he had a kid somewhere in the world who was taken away from him against his wishes and he had tried in vain to find. He's crazy smart, and super into politics, and always spouting off about something, but he'd also never made it through high school.

Even his name, like mine, isn't truly his. Despite the fact that it sounds Italian, he's actually full-blood Irish, but the name was misread by immigration when the family came over

years ago, and it stuck. And, of course, he'd struggled in-
tensely with addiction but had been clean for eleven years—
since he was a little older than I was. It was exactly the kind of
inspiration I needed. I asked him to be my sponsor, and, thankfully, he agreed.

Aside from our family backgrounds, our personal lives,
and our addictions, Chris and I also had something else major
in common—we were in the same business. He was a New
York restaurant veteran, with two decades of experience and a
solid following in the East Village. Years ago, he'd been the
executive chef at Lucky Cheng's, the campy drag Chinese place
that's become bachelorette party heaven. And for more than a
decade, he'd been the owner of the Oriental Grill, a casual
Asian fusion spot on 6th Street that everyone called O.G.

The nickname O.G. was appropriate, for it definitely was
one of the original gangstas of Americanized Pan Asian cuisine in New York—putting out dumplings and BBQ pork long
before there was a place on every corner doing the same thing.
But even though Chris was still popular and had a patronage
in the East Village that followed him around like he was Jesus
with a pair of chopsticks, Asian fusion was beginning to feel
like a fad gone wrong, and Chris thought it was time to get
back to basics.

After fifteen years in business, he was planning to close
O.G. that spring and open a new spot, which he was calling
6th Street Kitchen, in the same space. The Asian flavors would
be long gone—what Chris envisioned for his menu was classic
comfort food. The kind of food, he explained to me, that
you'd want to find in your mom's fridge, if your mom was the

best fucking cook in town. Meatballs. Roast chicken. That kind of thing. Plates could be ordered individually, but he encouraged a kind of communal dining—people ordering a bunch of things family style and eating together. I couldn't help but laugh when he told me his tagline: "Simple food for complicated people," a riff on an AA slogan.

Chris was my sponsor for most of the month of February, but even though things were great with him, I could tell that AA wasn't the right program for me. Aside from him, I didn't feel I was getting the support I needed, and knew that NA was probably a better fit for me in the long run. Chris encouraged me to go with my gut, and with his blessing, I officially fired him as my sponsor and went back to NA, knowing that in him, I'd at least found a friend and mentor.

But Chris had other plans for me. The morning after I fired him, he called and offered me a job. He needed an opening chef for 6th Street Kitchen, and he wanted me to do it.

It was exactly the kind of opportunity I was looking for— a real, steady job, but one that let me express myself through food, to put my own culinary stamp on something. To essentially—as I was in my personal life—start something completely fresh and new, totally from scratch. It felt like, for once, the two parallel paths in my life were running in the same direction—up.

Chris had already done most of the heavy lifting to get the restaurant open—he hired me at the end of February and was set to open the doors of 6th Street on April 1. He'd totally redesigned the O.G. space, making it match the homey, comforting concept he had in mind. It was a small place—it's hard not to be, in the East Village—but the open kitchen and long, communal tables made it feel bigger.

The whole place was redone in white wood, with simple white candles everywhere.

Rustic, but still totally elegant. He'd hired a start-up kitchen staff—mostly Mexican line cooks—and had started to get press rolling in. By the time I was on board, he'd even already had a Friends and Family Tasting.

So all I really had to do before we opened was to write a menu, and I couldn't wait. As long as I could remember, I'd sort of had food in the back of my mind, ideas for dishes and things I wanted to try, but since my birthday dinner at wd~50, it had turned into a full-blown obsession. I wanted to figure out how Dufresne had made every dish on his menu, and I wanted to replicate them, with my own twists on them. I had so many different flavor profiles in my mind that I would get up in the middle of the night and write them out maniacally before I forgot them, so I would wake up in the morning to a nightstand full of ingredient lists. There had never been a better time for me to write a menu.

But this wasn't the kind of menu I was dreaming about. This was supposed to be simple food. Home-cooked food. Food that people recognized and that reminded them of something, and not in the way the egg ravioli had reminded me of my childhood. This couldn't be a play on classic food. It had to actually be classic food. And Chris wasn't budging an inch on that.

I'd been talking to Chris about all of my experimental ideas for the last few months, but any time I made a suggestion for the menu that strayed from his concept, he shot me down, quickly and firmly. About a week before we opened, as I was putting the finishing touches on the menu, he came into the kitchen and said he wanted to have a chat, just to make sure we were on the same page.

We sat down on a pair of stools, and he began.

"I just want to let you know, first of all, how happy I am to have you on board. You're an incredibly talented guy, and Sixth Street is lucky to have you."

"I'm happy to be here, man. Really, I can't thank you enough."

"And I love hearing about all of the ideas you're having about food," he continued. "I get how excited you are, and I think it's great to see."

I nodded, knowing what was coming next.

"But I can't emphasize this enough. That's not the kind of food we're doing here. I want simple food. If you can't make it in a home kitchen, then we're not going to do it here."

"Okay, I got it," I said.

"Seriously, Brandon. I mean it. No agar. No xanthan gum. And I don't want to see a foam within a mile of this restaurant. Do you understand me?"

"Yeah, dude, I hear you."

And I did. But it didn't mean I wasn't disappointed. I was brimming with ideas, with ways to play around with the menu, with things I'd never done before.

But at the same time, Chris had a vision, and nothing I was going to say would change that. I knew how lucky I was to be there, and to have a boss like him. I told him I wasn't going to let him down, and I wouldn't.

So I opened 6th Street Kitchen the way Chris wanted. There was roast chicken, meatballs, deviled eggs, goat cheese croquettes, and little chorizo sliders. Pea soup with ham and garlic oil. Salmon with cauliflower and potatoes. Turnip confit, creamed Swiss chard, whipped potatoes, and polenta with mushrooms. For dessert, we were literally doing milk and cookies, and warm brownies with a ginger ice cream.

Part of me felt that Chris didn't have enough faith in people, thinking they would prefer a straight corn chowder to the same flavors done with a twist.

But I also knew that there was merit in what he was trying to do. With food that simple, it had to be done perfectly to be good. There weren't any smoke and mirrors to hide behind. It was just straight technique. If it wasn't done right, it wasn't going to be good. End of story. We had carrots on the menu— just plain carrots, cooked in champagne vinegar, veg stock, thyme, and garlic. Nothing complicated at all, but when they were done perfectly, and that mellow sweetness of the carrots caught the acid of the vinegar, I could've eaten ten fucking bowls of them.

After a month of intense prep on my part, and nearly a year on Chris's, we opened 6th Street Kitchen on April 1 to a great reception. The neighborhood had come out to support Chris, and the response to our simple, homey food was overwhelming. People loved it.

But on the second day, we were thrown a loop. For some reason, which I'm still not sure I understand, of all the guys that Chris had hired to work in the kitchen, only one, Luis, showed up again for work. So it was just the two of us that second night, pumping out food service for the whole restaurant. As stressful as it was, though, the night turned out to be an incredible blessing in disguise. The fact that all of the kitchen workers except Luis lost their jobs (even though, incredibly, a bunch had shown up the next day expecting to keep their jobs) meant that I, on Chris's direction, got to hire an entirely new staff.

I'd hired people before, but like almost everything else about the job, it felt different this time. I wasn't replacing just one guy here or there. I was building a team. For the first time, also, I started to understand why so many people had taken chances on me over the years, even though I hadn't been to culinary school or had the classic training that others might have. Hiring for a kitchen isn't only about experience, or even about talent. A lot of that can be learned. Hiring for a kitchen is about finding the right fit.

The day after the mass no-show, I started putting feelers out and began to assemble my staff. For my sous chef, I hired a dude named Dimitry Dinev, who had just graduated from the Culinary Institute of America, with a grand total of no actual chef experience under his belt. We bonded over the fact that he was a fellow Floridian, though the similarities ended there. His parents were Bulgarian and they were in the circus, literally—his mother was an elephant tamer, and his dad was on the trapeze. Dimitry probably wasn't going to be flying through the air with the greatest of ease anytime soon; he was a big lump of a guy with kind of an Eeyore voice to match. But I loved him. And, most important, he could cook.

∾

I started out with a pastry chef named Deek, a kind of old, boisterous meth head turned clean and sober with no teeth who used to sit around the kitchen and tell me crazy stories instead of cooking, so I had to let him go. I put out an ad to hire a new one, and when Jaimee Vitolo walked in, I knew she'd be perfect. She was friendly, and covered in tattoos, so we saw eye to eye right away. And I liked what she made for her tasting, too—a deconstructed strawberry rhubarb pie, with little circles of pâte brisée and a fruit compote—which convinced me that not only would she be fun to work with, but she also might be down to experiment in the kitchen some. We interviewed another pastry chef who had a lot more experience, but I knew from the beginning that Jaimee was our girl—it was all about the fit. To round things out, we also had Jorge, who I hired as our dishwasher after receiving a recommendation by someone I knew in NA, and Meghan, one of Chris's closest friends from AA who was already on board part-time before I got there.

Once I had my staff in place, my merry band of misfits, all we had to do was cook our asses off. From the very beginning, we were trying out new things all the time, tweaking the menu based on ingredients and mood and the way people reacted to our specials. With three to four distinct specials every night, we probably tried one hundred different new dishes in the first month alone. Reviews started coming in, and they confirmed what we had sensed from the crowds: It was going well. And we could breathe a little easier.

When we'd been open about two months, Chris told me to

take a long weekend off, to relax, and make sure I wasn't burning out. I had kept my commitment to sobriety, had stayed totally clean, but no one understood that struggle more than Chris. He knew that if I got too stressed, I could lose it all in a minute, and then we'd both be fucked.

Jacqueline's parents had a place upstate, in Bedford, New York, and so we planned a trip to see them, and I took along a copy of Thomas Keller's *French Laundry Cookbook*. I'd never been much into cookbooks before—I'd always been the kind of chef who learns as he goes along, picking up technique and recipes from different places where I worked. But as I got more and more interested in molecular gastronomy, it felt a little like I had to learn the basics all over again. I was dying to experiment at 6th Street, even in small ways, but before I could, I had to know what I was doing.

We were sitting outside in Jacqueline's parents' garden when, as I thumbed through the glossy pages, inspiration started to strike. Keller had a recipe for tomato sorbet, made with red wine vinegar and sautéed onions, that kept catching my eye. I loved the concept of a savory sorbet and wanted to try one but didn't want to rip off Keller. And suddenly, the scrambled egg ravioli appeared in my head again. The charred avocado. There had to be something there. I knew it was a little bit of a risk, given the conversation I'd had with Chris. But at least it wasn't a foam—and he hadn't said anything about sorbets. Hands itching, I picked up the phone, called 6th Street, asked for Dimitry, and read him the recipe, telling him to substitute avocados for the peeled tomatoes, and champagne vinegar for the red wine.

The next day, when we got back to the city, I picked up the avocado mixture from the freezer and ran it through the ice cream machine. It was cool, smooth, and insanely delicious. The high fat content in the avocados made it taste like ice cream, but the vinegar and sautéed onions made it undeniably savory. We served it that night on a brioche crouton with a little baby heirloom tomato salad, topped with ricotta salata and dressed with olive oil, vinegar, salt, and chive oil. And people went nuts.

With the first experiment a raging success, I started to branch out to other things. Since the avocado had gone so well, I tried another savory sorbet—feta, this time, with a watermelon-strawberry soup. We trotted it out as a special, and people were asking for it so often that I knew it would eventually have to end up on the permanent menu.

Jaimee was itching to shake things up on the pastry menu, too, so we started to collaborate on some new dishes. We did a Creamsicle panna cotta garnished with blackberry sorbet and seven different textures of pistachios, and another dish with Tootsie Rolls, buttermilk sherbet, poached cherries, and ganache. We were working on a lemon shortbread with a texture like a Fig Newton, and I wanted to pair it with a strawberry sorbet and a basil gel, but I kept running into a problem with the gel—the basil was turning brown, so it was not only unappealing but also lacked the surprise element that seemed so essential to the dish. I turned to Aki Kamozawa and Alexander Talbot's *Ideas in Food* to find out if there was a scientific solution to the problem, and started learning about liquid gel clarification. The gist is, if you add gelatin to your liquid, freeze it, and then slowly thaw it over cheesecloth, you end up with a clear gel with the essence of whatever flavor you were trying to capture. Exactly what I was looking for.

After that, things started to get out of hand. For one special, I encapsulated blueberries with clarified buttermilk gel and served them with little pieces of corn bread, and for another, I paired watermelon cubes in clarified juice with a fig balsamic gel. For a while, I basically wanted to turn everything I got my hands on into a gel. And an amazing thing started to happen with every new successful dish. I was starting to remember again why I loved cooking so much. It's easy to say that it was just a thing I fell into when I was a kid—that my mom owned a restaurant, or that I was too fidgety to do anything else. But there was a reason it had stuck when nothing else had. Now I felt I was really cooking the way I was meant to cook. With thought and passion and creativity. I was back in the game, for real.

But the deeper I got into this kind of cooking, the further I got from the restaurant Chris had opened, and he was definitely starting to notice.

One afternoon in the middle of June, I was working on a new amuse-bouche that I hoped to offer as a special that night, when Chris walked in.

"What's going on?" he asked, surveying the mess in front of me.

"Oh," I said, a little guiltily, "a one-bite Caesar salad amuse. I promise, you're going to love it. "

"What's in it?" he asked.

"A little brioche crouton," I said, starting to assemble one, "and pickled lemon, then this amazing clear romaine gel I just made, and parmesan gel. And anchovy—"

I stopped myself mid-sentence.

"Anchovy what, Brandon?"

"Foam."

"What did I tell you about foam?! There's no fucking foam in my kitchen!"

"Well," I admitted, and squirted some on top of the little salad Napoleon I'd just assembled, "actually there is now. But before you get pissed, just taste it."

He popped the bite into his mouth, chewed, and sighed.

"It's delicious, Brandon. But you know what it tastes like?"

"What?"

"A fucking Caesar salad! Why can't we just have that on the menu?"

"Because we're not the Olive Garden! People love this stuff! It's why they keep coming! It makes them actually think about their food in different ways!"

"But I didn't open the restaurant to make them think! I didn't hire you to make them think!"

"Then why did you hire me?"

"Because you're the best, most talented cook I know. And you don't need to hide behind any gimmicks to show that."

"Dammit," I said, slamming down the mold, "so you really just want me to make sliders and roast chicken for the rest of my life?"

"No. But if you make the best roast chicken and the best sliders in the city, doesn't that count for something?"

"It does, but it's also fucking boring! We can do things here that no one else is doing!"

"I know you're on your way to that. And I'm proud as hell of you. But it's not going to happen all at once."

"Fine. So what do you want me to do with this amuse now?"

"Oh, just leave it on there for tonight. I guess it's just an amuse. And, hey, you might be right about this one," he said, smiling a little as he walked back into the dining room. "But in the future, I'm serious about the foam."

I felt like I had won, even if it was just a little victory, just for the night. And part of me knew that Chris was right. I didn't always need smoke and mirrors, gels and foams, sorbets and liquid nitrogen. It was always going to be more important to cook something the right way and combine the right flavors and make things taste good. I didn't want my dishes to haunt people in the same way the scrambled egg ravioli haunted me—making me think but at the expense of making the dish actually work.

At the same time, I was excited—really pumped, actually—about cooking for the first time in as long as I could remember. I was glad that Chris sometimes let me have my way, like with the amuse that night. And I knew that, in his own small way, he was letting me use 6th Street to figure out who I was as a chef. But now that I was starting to figure out that, as much as I loved him and loved 6th Street, there was also a part of me that wanted more than anything not just to sneak in little experimental bites here and there, but to be doing it every single night.

We served the amuse that night, and just as I had hoped,

people were talking about it all night. Chris came into the kitchen at the end of service, rolling his eyes, but slapped his hand on my back and congratulated me for officially fucking with the heads of all his customers.

Jacqueline was still up when I got home, and I couldn't wait to tell her about it—the dish, the fight with Chris, ideas for what I wanted to try next. I had so many things in my head, so many concepts for dishes swirling around. I wanted to hear what she thought, but she was quiet as I talked, uncharacteristically so. Just kept rubbing my back and thinking.

Finally, she spoke up.

"I know you love Sixth Street. But there might be a chance for you to do all that. And more."

"What do you mean?"

"I heard at work tonight that Grant Achatz is hiring at Alinea."

I laughed.

"Alinea? Like, three-Michelin-star Alinea?"

"That's the one."

"Not a chance."

"What do you mean?"

"It's fucking Alinea! They could have anyone they wanted. Why would they even look twice at someone like me?"

But even as I said it, my mind was swirling. It was definitely a long shot. But, God, what if they did call me in?

"Don't sell yourself short," she said. "You've got a kick-ass resume and serious talent. And if this is the kind of food you want to be doing, you owe it to yourself to try."

"Yeah, but I love Sixth Street," I said, and that was true.

Sixth Street had become like a family to me, and Chris was the best boss I'd ever had. "I can't leave Chris."

"You wouldn't be leaving him in a lurch. You'd find him a replacement. And Chris knows just as well as you do that you're not going to be at Sixth Street forever."

That, also, I knew was true. For all we bickered about the stupid little things, mostly Chris left me alone. Not only because he trusted me and knew I was doing right by his restaurant. But also because he was letting me work out whatever kinks I needed to work out before I moved on to bigger places. He wanted me to stay. I'm sure of that. But he also knew that eventually, I was going to move on, and he wanted, in the best way possible, to let me use his kitchen to figure out how I would do that.

And it was fucking Alinea. I hadn't eaten there yet, but I knew from reputation that it was shifting boundaries, reimagining food in exactly the ways that interested me. Jacqueline was right. If that was ultimately the kind of food I wanted to do, it was worth giving it a try. Sixth Street was home, but I had to grow up sometime.

I sent in my resume the next morning and, much to my shock, received a response via e-mail from the chef de cuisine, Dave Beran, a day later. They were impressed with what they saw, and wanted me to come in to stage as soon as I could get to Chicago.

Jacqueline and I each asked for a few days off work and booked tickets right away. It felt like a double win. Even if nothing ended up happening with Alinea, it would be amazing to eat there, to cook in their kitchen for a couple of days, to see what happened behind the scenes. And we'd both get a little vacation, a break from New York.

My life was better than it had been in years. I was clean, had a great job, a stable and supportive relationship. What made the idea of leaving all of that so appealing? I can't say that, at the particular moment, I knew I was pursuing the right path for my life, but I do know that my life in New York had reached a plateau. Had I stayed in New York, I know without a doubt that I would be that stick-up-my-ass sober chef with no further aspirations. But Alinea presented me new goals—and the risk of losing what I had worked toward for the last eight months of my life.

CHAPTER SEVEN

All my life, people have told me that I'm like a cat—fearless, and with more lives to work with than everyone else. Personally, I kind of think cats are suckers if they only get nine. I'm only twenty-eight now—just a quarter of my way through, if you're feeling optimistic—and I feel like I've already used up way more than my fair share. I'm not talking about close calls or accidents or any of that shit, though I'm no stranger to those, either. What I mean is reinvention—times when I've changed, fundamentally, who I am, for better or for worse. And at no time has that felt more apparent than the year I turned twenty-five.

It was July when I had this epiphany, six months into my first quarter century kicking around on Earth, and I remember the moment so clearly I can tell you the exact date: July 8, 2010. Around one A.M. I had just finished my first night staging at Alinea, and I was sitting in the alley in the back of the restaurant, smoking a cigarette and looking up at the Chicago skyline and praying to some unknown god up there that I wouldn't fuck this one up.

It was one of those perfect Chicago nights. The kind that, I'd later realize, makes you almost forget the hell the city puts you through all winter. I'd arrived three days earlier, and it'd been nothing but blue skies and sunshine since then.

Summer nights in New York felt sticky, like someone had thrown a giant, mildewed towel over the city. But even though it was still warm in the middle of the night in Chicago, there was an amazing breeze coming in from the lake that made the hot air feel crisp somehow.

I lit another cigarette, without taking my eyes off the sky. The buildings were so tall here, they made even New York look like a bunch of ant farms. If there was a god anywhere, maybe he was up there, hopping from rooftop to rooftop, laughing at all of us assholes on the ground. I squinted up at them, thinking about all the mistakes I'd made, all the dumb shit I'd done, all the times I'd taken chances and screwed them up. If I tried really hard, could I make this one different?

The doors to Alinea swung open behind me, and a few cooks came stumbling out, still in clogs and chef's pants. I jumped up at the noise and got up and out of their way as they brushed past me and started to make their way into the alley.

"Hey, man," one of them called out, turning back to look at me, "you were staging tonight, right? Doing the lobster skewers on vanilla beans?"

I nodded.

"What's your name?"

"Brandon. Brandon Baltzley."

"Well, Brandon Baltzley, we're going to get some drinks over at the Black Duck. They're open for another hour." He paused. "And we know a guy there."

I looked at him, but didn't say anything. I can't say I wasn't tempted. I didn't know a soul in this city. Didn't have a thing to do but sit out in the alley and look at the goddamn skyscrapers all night.

"So, you in?"

"Nah, man," I managed to make myself say, "I'm cool."

They walked away and I sat down on the stoop again and looked back up at the buildings. Take that, God, you tricky motherfucker.

One test passed.

A year ago, I'd have gotten up and followed them wherever they were going without any questions asked.

But a year ago, I wouldn't have been here at all.

On July 4, 2010, Jacqueline and I left JFK at six A.M., headed for Chicago. The sun was just starting to rise above the wing of the plane, and we had a perfect view of the Manhattan skyline as we took off. It looked so tiny, outlined in the water of New York Harbor—it was almost hard to believe that so much shit had gone down on such a little island.

As the plane ascended, I could feel the anticipation build in my stomach, thinking about everything we had planned for the weekend. We had a reservation that night at Alinea, and the next day we were going to Tru, followed by Schwa. And these wouldn't be ordinary meals, either—the "culinary liaison" at Per Se had made the Alinea reservation, and Grant Achatz had made the one at Schwa. In other words, not only were we going to the two best restaurants in Chicago, but we'd be getting special treatment at both.

We checked into the Blake Hotel, a nice little place on Dearborn Street in the South Loop that, I'd later find out, was home to a decent restaurant called Custom House, and we only had a few hours to rest and get ready to head out to Alinea. I wasn't much for dressing up—at that time, I had hair that fell below my shoulders, and a big, unruly beard. But I could fake it well enough in dress slacks, a button-up shirt, and a jacket. Jacqueline put on a blue dress, and she looked good. As we left the hotel room, I caught a glimpse of us in the mirror. We looked normal, on the verge of happy, even. I couldn't believe how far we'd come.

We took the Red Line "L" train to the North/Clybourn stop and walked over to Alinea, and I got more and more excited with every step. I felt like Alinea had been in my dreams ever since my dinner at wd~50 the previous year, and I'd done everything I could to prepare for it. I'd watched YouTube videos of the dishes being prepared, hitting the refresh button over and over again. I'd cooked nearly everything I could from Alinea's cookbook. I'd subjected Chris and my cooks at 6th Street Kitchen to a nonstop barrage about Alinea. I thought I was prepared for every surprise they had coming. But Alinea still managed to sweep me off my feet.

Even the layout of the restaurant was a study in contrast. We entered through a long, dimly lit hallway that felt to me a little like a personal drug den. It actually reminded me of a neon-lit nook I made in my own bedroom growing up, to escape the day-to-day life of a teenager. Then, at the very end of the hall, on the left, double doors shot open at what seemed like the speed of sound, scaring the shit out of me. And then we were in the dining room, a big, warm, open room exactly the opposite of the hallway entrance.

We were immediately greeted by a redheaded man with a bow tie and beard, who called me Chef and told me that Chef Achatz was planning to serve us the larger of the two tasting menus. (Alinea has only one menu now, but at the time, they had a twelve-course and a twenty-six-course tasting menu.) The server also had informed us that we would both have a beverage pairing, mine nonalcoholic since I had opted for the no-raw-alcohol preference. This was surprising; I had thought, through my research, that Alinea didn't offer such a thing. Jacqueline, who, for support, hadn't drunk alcohol in probably seven months, was given a full-blown wine pairing.

And then we began. The meal started with a frozen English pea mousse served inside a rocks glass along with ham, olive oil, and mint. None of the ingredients was in a standard form. The olive oil was frozen in a square, the mint was a clear gel, and the ham was an ice. It was fucking delicious. I tried to wrap my mind around the different techniques of the first course, but it proved nearly impossible. I went into this experience wanting to know everything about what Alinea was doing, but I had no inkling of what was going on. I couldn't stop staring at the flag hanging from a custom-made service piece in the middle of the black, perfectly square table.

It looked almost edible. Four courses later, the mystery was solved: It was to be used as a spring roll wrapper for a Thai-style coconut curry with fatty pork belly and a line of maybe nine garnishes including fried garlic, parisienned cucumbers, red pepper pudding, Hawaiian black sea salt, raw red onion, mixed micro herbs, compressed mango, and lime segments.

Nearly every dish of the twenty-six we ate that night was memorable, everything complex and imaginative and inspiring. But some in particular stood out. There was the salad course of raw, whole baby vegetables, complete with stems and leaves, then dusted with "ranch" powder, and an oxalis and honey one-bite course so perfectly balanced in flavor and texture that I wanted go home and burn my clogs and trash my knives and give up cooking altogether. The whole extravaganza crescendoed to a finale with Grant Achatz coming to the table and plating a chocolate, coconut, and menthol dish on the table. The "dish" was so large that we couldn't finish it. I can't even remember the exact components of the dish since I was so full my mind wasn't functioning to capacity. When we completed our meal, our server told us she was not to accept any form of payment from us. The thought that we just consumed about six hundred dollars' worth of food and beverage and were not going to have to pay for it blew us away. I think that was the first time I realized what kind of pull working in a Michelin-starred restaurant had. They wouldn't even let us leave a tip.

We both left with full stomachs, and a few stars floating in our eyes. Jacqueline could blame the alcohol, but for the first time in my life, I felt drunk on food, and on possibility. I couldn't believe that, in a few days, I'd be going back to cook that very same food.

But our holiday weekend was only just beginning. The next day, with more cash in our pockets than we'd expected, we ended up at Tru. Anthony Martin, a chef who had worked his way through exclusive Las Vegas dining establishments, had just taken over as chef, and I wanted to see what he was up to. The first thing I noticed was the impeccable service. Our waitress was elegant, classy, and attractive, and she ended up becoming my first informant about the weird world of the Chicago food scene and its inhabitants. At the beginning of the meal, she'd asked us why we were in town, and when we told her I'd be staging at Alinea, she made it her business to tell me what was what. And not all of it was what I wanted to hear, two days before my stage started. "Stage there," she said, "if picking herbs and vacuuming floors are things you enjoy."

Nonetheless, I tried to keep my nerves at bay and focus on the food at Tru. I wasn't disappointed, but after the performance at Alinea the night before, this couldn't even begin to compare. The technique was spot-on, but there wasn't a whole lot of creativity. And everything seemed to need salt. The most interesting part of the meal was the pastry course, when I tried osmanthus, a Japanese wildflower tea, for the first time. It was flavor so unusual that it's difficult even to articulate, but it was something that would come back and haunt my taste buds over and over again in years to come, eventually finding its way onto my menus on multiple occasions.

When I come across a new flavor, something I have never

tasted before, it excites me in a way only a four-year-old child would understand. By that point, it felt as if I had tasted almost everything. Sure, there were new and interesting ways to combine flavors, and exciting techniques. But to discover an entirely new flavor felt revolutionary. Things like osmanthus, pawpaw, acorn, and pine awoke things inside that had felt dead for quite some time.

What I didn't know yet at that point was that Chicago would be the epicenter of a lot of this kind of discovery for me over the next few years. There was clearly a creative boom happening in the food world of Chicago. L2O, Alinea, Schwa, Tru, Graham Elliot, Longman & Eagle—they were all doing things on a plane different from most New York restaurants. Of course, New York had Corton and wd~50. But I'd seen all that shit already. I'd eaten there and studied them and soaked in what I could. Now I needed to move on.

Finally, on my fourth day in Chicago, I would get that chance. I was starting my stage at Alinea. And I was nervous as hell. Standing in the alley behind the restaurant, I closed my eyes and said a quick prayer to who knows what that I wouldn't fuck this up. And then I heard footsteps in the alley behind me, and saw a clean-cut man open the door in front of me and walk in. I knew from his picture on the website that he was the sous, and that it was my cue to get started.

Alinea gives three choices for stages for the most part. Anyone who is there for a two-day stage is trying out for a paid position. Anyone there for a weeklong stage is usually employed elsewhere and just wants to hang out in the kitchen for a week. People have also been known to do a season at

Alinea. These could last anywhere from three to six months, from what I understood, and most people who did them were from other countries. I was there for a two-day stage, because I was staging for a full-time position at Alinea.

I was instructed by Matt Chasseur to go downstairs and put on a chef's jacket, leave my knife roll downstairs, and bring back a peeler, paring knife, and chef knife. When I came back upstairs, I was told to walk across the kitchen and pick up a roll-up, which consisted of three towels and an apron. This was definitely foreign territory—I was used to being able to use my own tools, even when staging. It was rather unsettling to have completely foreign tools to work with when you were vying for a job at one of the most respected restaurants on the continent.

It's common practice among kitchen professionals to wear a blue apron during prep and change into a white one when service begins. But even that was different at Alinea, where everyone wore long, white bistro aprons that went from waist to ankle. I fucking hated the things. I never saw the point in an apron that didn't have a bib. The only thing I hate worse are cooks who take a perfectly good bib apron and fold it under. The apron has a bib for a reason; it shouldn't be tucked under. That's the equivalent of sagging your pants.

There were about five stagiaires, but I only remember two—a kid from Denmark and one from Minnesota—because the other three didn't make it past the first day. They assigned me to work with Nell, a chef de partie who had just been promoted to a tournant, which turned out to be incredibly lucky. She was super nice to me, and patient with me, which, I quickly learned, was pretty rare. For the most part, as it turns out, everyone who cooks at Alinea is a raging fucking prick. You can be doing something correctly and someone, somewhere, will hone in on what you are doing and figure out a way to tell you you're a piece of shit for doing it the wrong way. Then three other cooks will give you a different, "better" way to do the task, then the sous chef will yell at you and tell you that you are an even bigger piece of shit and that you "don't belong in the number one restaurant in the country." The task in question? Taking out the garbage. It was like being a pinball and getting pinged from asshole to asshole. The military atmosphere of the kitchen was the perfect way for the chefs to vet the candidates they needed for the positions they had open.

Even though it wasn't the best working environment, I really enjoyed making the food on my station. I was responsible for three dishes: a lobster, gruyere, and lychee skewered on a vanilla bean and then tempura-fried; a distillation of Thai flavors including lemongrass, bird chile, and basil; and a pork belly spring roll dish. The spring roll, I was thrilled to find out, was the same one that involved the dramatic flag centerpiece as a wrapper, which had caught my attention during the tasting menu a couple of days before.

The day was long and intense—fourteen hours of literally running from one place to another, with only a thirty-minute break for family meal. I was used to long shifts and hard work, but there was something particularly draining about this, knowing how much I wanted to impress the staff, who seemed to be impossible to impress, and feeling so close to a dream.

It finally ended and I went back to the hotel, exhausted but excited. Jacqueline was waiting up for me, and started to rub my feet and ask me how it went. But I was out like a light before I could tell her about the three-towel rule, an exacting practice that allowed the use of only three towels for the entire service in an effort to maintain cleanliness.

I slept better than I had in years, and woke up and immediately got my shit ready to go out the door for the second day. This time I knew I needed to get something in my stomach before going into work. I stopped at the Borders on North and Clybourn and ordered the closest thing to my favorite NYC breakfast, an egg on a roll, that I could find. I downed it with a green drink and an iced coffee and began my one-block walk with my cigarette to Alinea's back door.

I felt calm on the second day, and more comfortable in my surroundings. I was already moving more quickly than I did normally. I knew where things were, which had been an issue the day before. It's always difficult to start out in a new kitchen without knowing the lay of the land, but at Alinea, it seemed as if they kept things hidden on purpose. There were two long passes on either side of the kitchen, underneath where we plated food, and that's where we kept trash cans, hydrocolloids, spices, plates, tools, and containers. All the heavier-duty equipment, like anti-griddles, circulators, and vaporizers, were housed down a flight of stairs and through the employee bathroom/laundry/locker rooms in a crawl space. Carrying shit in and out of a crawl space can be a huge pain in the dick. Especially when you're over four feet tall.

At four P.M. we broke for family meal, which was a hell of

an ordeal. Everything would have to be cleaned for the third time that day, since kitchens of this echelon take regular cleaning rituals to maintain them. And I'm not talking just wiping things off. I mean a total fucking end-of-the-night breakdown. No one gives a fuck what you are working on or where you are at in its progress. All that matters is that you better get that shit put away, scrub your station, and immediately get on either dishes or floors. Dishwashers? There aren't any fucking dishwashers at Alinea until service starts.

The process was a pain, but it also meant that everyone had to work smart, and that was something I picked up quickly. I couldn't use any unnecessary containers, because I'd end up having to wash them all. I had to know my mise en place. I had to know that, through the entire day on the pork belly station, I would need two saucepots: one for frying my tempura, and one to make my coconut curry. I'd need a spoon bain, two induction burners, a quarter sheet pan, a large mixing bowl to soak the rice paper in yuzu, a handful of plastic deli containers, spoons, and, depending on the day, a Vita Prep to puree the red-pepper-agar-fluid gel for the pork belly set. If I didn't get to these things first, there would be no guarantee they would be around at the exact moment I needed them. And that could be disastrous.

Nell's station was working a little ahead of schedule, so they moved me one station over to what I guess you would call the meat station, since it was responsible for a beef and lamb course, though in a kitchen that conceptual, it was a little difficult to make conventional distinctions. The kid working there had a completely ridiculous fauxhawk and looked like a

Park Slope lesbian, and he gave me a few tasks to do for his two plates.

The beef course was very simple, which was a taste of what was to come at Achatz's new restaurant, Next. It was a recipe straight from Escoffier: beef, tomato, banana, tarragon, foie-and-rice-stuffed pepper, demi-glace. But the lamb course was totally different, and, even though there was a lot of competition, I'm pretty sure it was the coolest dish on the menu.

A lot of chefs claim to tell stories on their plates, but Alinea's lamb dish actually did just that. During my dinner a few days earlier, the chef had told me that he was inspired by a visit to Elysian Fields Farm, in Pennsylvania, where he'd gone after taking a particular liking to their lamb. Wanting to put the meat back in its idyllic habitat, he actually configured the plate and all its elements to look like the rolling hills where the animals were raised. The lamb itself was a piece of sous vide loin, which was skewered on a rosemary sprig and placed on a babbling brook of popcorn soup. Then there was a seventy-two-hour sous vide lamb belly, which was picked into individual threads, rolled into little balls, and deep-fried. When we put them in the dehydrator, they looked just like little hay bales. Finally, there was huckleberry, to which we added agar and then dropped that mixture, while hot, out of a squeeze bottle into liquid nitrogen to form little huckleberry bush spheres. Excessive, I know, but shit was dope.

There was one more element to the lamb dish. It started with a parsley sheet, and they wanted it cut to look like grass. I have no idea how they managed to make a parsley sheet in the first place, though I assume it involved blending parsley juice with Ultra-Tex and then dehydrating it on acetate sheets. The only instruction I was given was to "julienne this." So I did. Apparently, my julienne was slightly larger than the julienne the chef wanted and that is when I had my first run-in with Matthew Chasseur, a man who seemingly took leadership lessons from Kim Jong-il.

Chasseur quickly walked over to me and whispered tensely: "What the fuck is this, Chef?"

"He told me to julienne the paper," I replied. "I didn't know what size."

"You don't just do things you don't know how to do," he shot back. "You're in the number one restaurant in the country, Chef. This is shit. Go downstairs and cut each one of these 'blades of grass' in half. And get it done quickly. I don't think you want to miss service when you're trying out for a job."

"Yes, Chef," I said, and quickly ran downstairs and began cutting each fucking piece of the fucking parsley paper in half. It was like one thousand blades. It was bullshit. Especially because he wouldn't end up using it at all. But that was my punishment. I had to spend time laboring over something he knew he was going to throw away anyway.

Every thirty to forty-five minutes or so, Chasseur would pop down and remind me why I was there, slinging humiliating insults at me: "I bet you won't do that again" or "Chef, you better hurry up if you actually want a job here."

Around eight P.M. he finally returned and grabbed all of the grass and threw it away and told me to go up to the meat station. I'd be lying if I said the guy didn't make me tear up a bit. Not at the fact that he was mean, but at the complete frustration I was feeling about being misinstructed by someone and then being punished, in a completely degrading way, for someone else's fuckup. To be honest, I wasn't really used to giving that much of a shit. But I wanted this job more than I'd wanted anything in a long time. I could tell that these were the kinds of chefs I wanted to work with. And to have it feel that tantalizingly close was nerve-racking as hell.

I spent the rest of the evening helping out on the meat station, plating some lamb plates, while Chasseur stood on the opposite side of the pass plating the beef course. I still feel a little nauseous when I think of how I spent that night, glaring at him and trying to read his face. Was he going to screw me over? Or was he going to give me a chance?

Looking back on it now, I doubt that Chasseur is actually that much of a prick in real life. But seeing how he acted that night gave me just a little taste of what it could be like in the kitchen of one of the world's most watched restaurants. This was the fucking pinnacle of fine dining, of cutting-edge cuisine. And that meant that, in the kitchen, it was survival of the fittest. I'd like to think that Chasseur treated people the way he did to fill a role. Beran, who was the chef de cuisine, and Graves, the junior sous, were serious but rational, nice guys on the whole. So maybe Chasseur knew there had to be someone busting balls. And once I became immune to it, it wasn't always that bad. There never really seemed like much of a reason why you were being verbally skull-fucked by Chasseur, but you can bet your ass, when it wasn't you taking the pounding, the shit that would come out of that guy's mouth was pretty hysterical.

As service was wrapping up that night, Chef Beran

brought me and the kid from Minneapolis outside to the alley and told us simply, "You guys did a good job the past two days. If you want jobs, you've got them at Alinea."

I did a fucking double take. I couldn't believe what I was hearing. I had thought I had done a completely shit job that night, and now I was being handed the opportunity of a life-time. It was all I could do to keep from hugging the bastard.

The Minnesotan must have been feeling the same way because we both just stood there with blank faces, looking at Beran and waiting for what came next. He continued on with the details—a $26,500-a-year salary, plus two weeks' paid vacation a year, two weeks of holiday when the restaurant would be closed, and insurance that was available at full cost in the beginning but would get cheaper the longer we stayed, then completely free after the first year. It wasn't a lot of money, but in my head I was thinking it couldn't get much better. Most Michelin-starred restaurants pay even worse and certainly don't have benefits or paid vacation. I almost couldn't believe what I was hearing.

The Minnesotan said he could begin work in two weeks, but I knew I needed a little more time, given my situation at 6th Street Kitchen. I was not only employed there, but also a partner. I paused for a minute and explained to Chef Beran that I would need a full month before I returned. He agreed and sent us on our way. The Minnesotan and I jogged down the blue concrete staircase, and when we knew we were out of sight from anyone, we simultaneously looked at each other and did what could only be described as a fist pump. We had jobs at Alinea.

I changed my clothes and headed back to the hotel to tell Jacqueline the great news. I was so excited I could barely keep an even stride. My heart was racing and I was out of breath. Finally, after years of misses, I felt like I was where I really needed to be to move up in my career.

But as I left Alinea to get a cab, my stomach started to churn, and I realized there was a downside to the news, and it was impossible to ignore. I was proud of myself for what I'd achieved. But I also couldn't ignore the fact that I had let my drive come before the two most important people in my life, both of whom were in New York. One, a loving and committed partner and the other a friend, mentor, and ally. Both Jacqueline and Chris had been there for me in my darkest times and lifted me up, at times literally, and made me the person I was that day. And now I had to be prepared to leave them both. This was going to be far more complicated than I thought.

Even though Jacqueline knew what was going on and was supportive and happy for me, telling Chris and everyone at 6th Street was going to be a different story. And I didn't quite know how I was going to do it. When our plane landed at LaGuardia the next day, I took a cab straight from the airport to the East Village and headed for Sixth Street. It was probably four in the afternoon and Dimitry, Meghan, Chris, and Jaimee were all hammering out prep for service, and Chris was standing around the kitchen, flipping through a cookbook. I acted as if nothing had changed. I gave everyone a hug and began to tell them all the things I saw in Chicago—the buildings, the people, the food. The fucking food. That could get me through at least a day.

I put all my things downstairs and got changed into my porter shirt for service. It felt I was being deceitful, but at that point, even I wasn't sure if I was going to take the job at Alinea. For the first time in a really long time, maybe ever, things had started to become consistent in my life. I had an apartment with Jacqueline on the Upper West Side, I had a very well paying job, and everyone I knew, my entire support system, was in New York. The closest thing to friends that I had in Chicago were old bands I had previously toured with while I was playing with Kylesa, and I had no idea how to reach them.

I knew what to do: I had another stage set up the following Tuesday. It wasn't a job I had been particularly excited about, or even one that I had knowingly applied for. Long before 6th Street Kitchen came to fruition, I had uploaded my resume to a culinary job searching website called starchefs .com, and I guess it had just been sitting there for the past year, collecting the Internet's cobwebs. As I was obsessively mulling over the job offer from Alinea, a call came from a sous chef from The Inn at Little Washington. He had found my resume and was in need of a tournant. It wasn't Alinea, and probably wasn't right for me. But, over the phone, the chef said that if I drove down to do the stage, he would put me and Jacqueline up for the night in their inn. All I had to do was bring my knives and clogs. Maybe, I figured, it would give me the peace of mind and buy me another two days to figure out what I really wanted.

Jacqueline and I borrowed a car from her parents in up-state New York and made the six-hour trek to Washington,

Virginia, a couple of hours south of DC. I'd heard a lot about The Inn at Little Washington during my time in DC—it had been around forever, and specialized in classical French cooking—but I'd never been there, largely because it was in the middle of fucking nowhere.

As we approached on a winding country road, our cell phones lost signals, the air got thick, and the greenery of the pastures looked more like Ireland than Virginia. It was absolutely beautiful, but hard to believe we were even in the same country as New York City. We parked, and walked through the lobby to find a handful of women dressed in French maid outfits. I don't think I'd ever seen one that wasn't on a stripper pole or at a Halloween party. Unfortunately, these weren't the sexy kind, but the classic one. Complete with bonnets and the calloused look of age. They looked like they hadn't had a day off their entire lives.

I told them I was there to stage and they showed me the restaurant. I was already rolling my eyes in disbelief at the place when the sous who had recruited me came out of the office in the most ridiculous fucking chef pants I had ever seen: baggy, Dalmatian-printed chef's pants. He also had a matching skullcap/bandanna thing that clung to his head like a cheap, too-small condom.

He told me to put my knives in the office and he would get me suited up in their uniform. *Fan-fucking-tastic*, I thought. As he took me into an area where the cooks kept their lockers, he handed me a hat, pants, and jacket. Jacqueline was getting a brief tour of the kitchen, and the sous and I returned to the area where I had dropped my knife roll. All of a sudden, a blond woman in a pantsuit emerged from another office, holding a business card in her left hand while extending her right to shake my hand. She looked sort of disturbed. But I couldn't possibly have prepared myself for what came out of her mouth.

"I'm very sorry to have to say this, but we can't have you working or even staging here with your visible tattoos," she said. "We feed politicians and have a kitchen table, and your tattoos are against our company policy. We would like to give you a bag of cookies to take with you on your return trip to New York City, though." And the chefs in the vicinity didn't even blink an eye.

Needless to say, Jacqueline and I were taken aback. I thought this was 2010, for fuck's sake. Apparently, I was mistaken. Washington, Virginia: the town that time forgot. We had just driven more than six hours to get there, only to be turned away at first glance. They didn't even give us the hotel room they'd promised on the phone—we were there barely ten minutes and had to get right back in the car and start driving again. I guess manners are lost that close to the Mason-Dixon Line.

So, in one day, we drove twelve hours for a bag of shitty cookies. Yeah, they weren't even good. I thought I was mad, but Jacqueline was furious: "My fucking sous chef at Per Se has *FOIE GRAS* tattooed on his knuckles!"

I was honestly baffled. I didn't have much to say. But I suppose the trip had served its original purpose: It gave me separation from New York and Chicago, and a lot of time to think. I sat quietly in the car as we drove through the hills of Virginia, and lost myself in a spiral of self-deprecating thoughts—tattoos, substance problems, addiction to sex with strange women, a mentality of survival and will to succeed that could end in an untimely death. If I let them, these things could take me over. They could outweigh even what I did best: cooking and pounding out a beat on the drums. So, in the end, the mentality for survival trumped thoughts of addiction and promiscuity, and I made the difficult decision that I would return to NYC and tell Chris that I would be leaving in one month for the job that was offered to me by Alinea.

I returned to work the following day. It wasn't ideal to begin with. I hadn't told Chris about the trip to Little Washington, and when he found out that I'd taken the day off, he was pissed. For the past five months, I had worked seven-day workweeks. He had to almost beg me to take a rest. So he knew that when I abruptly started taking days off, especially without asking him, something had to be going on.

After dinner, Chris sat me down at the dining-room table closest to my station in our open kitchen, and asked me what was up. I knew he was looking out for his restaurant, but the concern in his eyes told me that he was looking out for me, too, which made it a little bit easier. I took a deep breath and explained to him the situation. I explained that I wanted to go to Chicago to work at Alinea. I explained that it wasn't quite planned out and the opportunity had come as a surprise to me. I explained that it was not personal—the opposite of it, in fact—that it pained me to leave him and the amazing place we had built together, but that I had to do it for self-improvement. And I explained that I wasn't going to leave him in a lurch. That I wanted to help find and train my replacement and leave

6th Street Kitchen in the best possible set of hands I could find. It shouldn't have surprised me that Chris, as he always has been, was nothing but understanding and supportive.

And the next day, the whirlwind started. In the course of a month, I had to find an apartment in Chicago, plan my move almost a third of the way across the country, and find a new chef for 6th Street Kitchen. None of these tasks proved easy. I interviewed a variety of candidates for the chef position, including a Michelin two-star-rated chef de cuisine. Chris and I eventually settled on one of Ryan Skeen's boys, Greg Torrech and his sous chef, Andrew Kraft, freshly on the market from Allen & Delancey after its closing. They seemed to have an understanding of exactly what Chris wanted for 6th Street Kitchen's menu. I stayed on for about three more weeks, one of them including a side-by-side with Greg and Andrew. They were commendable cooks and considerate professionals. I knew they would do well.

But something else was going on. Three weeks into the stress of planning my move to Chicago, I felt a small, painful bump behind my left ear. It felt like someone was injecting a needle into the side of my head. I asked Chris to look at it and give me his opinion. He suggested that I go to the doctor, but I ignored him. I fucking hate doctors, and anyway, there wasn't time, given all the loose ends I had to tie up before moving. The following day, though, three more red bumps appeared on the left side of my head, and I was out of options.

I walked into the examination room and told the doctor what was going on. He put on a pair of latex gloves and tilted my head to the side. Immediately, he asked me if I had ever gotten chickenpox. I was confused, but I told him that I had, when I was six years old.

He looked straight at me and said, "You, sir, have shingles."

I couldn't believe my luck. The stress of the job, move, and relationships, coupled with my propensity for damaging my body, had stricken me with shingles at the age of twenty-five. This meant I couldn't return to work, which was a bit of a devastating blow. Believe me, I tried. Chris wasn't having it. Not only had I wanted to stay on to make sure it was a smooth transition in the kitchen, but 6th Street was my home. To feel exiled from them on my last days in the city was torture.

The only silver lining to getting shingles was that I had more time during that last week to spend with my friends and with Jacqueline. She had stood by me through the whole process, and while she was, of course, sad to see me go, we were determined that we could make it work long-distance. I still felt conflicted about leaving her for Chicago, especially since she'd been so important to helping me through the last year, but together we had come to the conclusion that this was an opportunity I couldn't pass up.

I spent my last night in town at Nate Appleman's old digs, Pulino's, on the Bowery. There was a table of fourteen, and we ate pizza and shelled mussels and laughed and told stories. Some drank beer while plenty of others, also struggling to stay clean, stuck to soda. It was a perfect night, surrounded by people I loved and cherished, but also extremely bittersweet. I knew I was making a good decision, but, feeling so content with my surroundings, it was impossible to imagine why the fuck I would even consider leaving them all. I wished I could stop the clock, just for a minute, to preserve that feeling of peace and comfort, knowing that tomorrow, everything would change.

I hugged everyone's necks and felt teary inside, then returned with Jacqueline to our apartment on the Upper West Side and finished packing my bags. I woke up at five the next morning, said good-bye to Jacqueline, and took a communal taxi to the airport. I held my head up high, but in some ways, I had never felt more alone in my life. I had no idea what lay ahead, or if I was strong enough to confront it on my own. I only had nine months of sobriety under my belt, which I had worked harder at than anything in my life. In three weeks, that sobriety would be gone. And along with it, so would Jacqueline.

CHAPTER EIGHT

I arrived in Chicago at ten forty-five on a Saturday morning. The date was August 14, 2010, and all I remember is that it was way too hot to be wearing a fucking suit. We Southerners are raised to "dress up" when flying somewhere. Don't ask me why; I couldn't tell you, but it's just a thing I used to do.

I hailed a cab to my new apartment in the Wrigleyville neighborhood. Because I'd had to move so suddenly, and without knowing jack shit about Chicago, I had picked the place blindly—I knew nothing about the neighborhood, hadn't seen the apartment, and hadn't met my new roommate. All I knew was that six hundred dollars for a shared, two-bedroom apartment seemed more than reasonable after moving out of my two-thousand-dollar one-bedroom on the Upper West Side.

I quickly found out that this was not the neighborhood for me. Anyone who has ever lived in Chicago knows to avoid

Wrigleyville like the motherfucking plague. I mean, unless you like date rape coupled with frat boys puking on streets and pissing in people's faces.

As I walked up the four flights of stairs, I wasn't terribly optimistic. But, I thought, at least it wasn't all that much different from New York City. You spend money to get home and then you practically climb a mountain to get inside your un-air-conditioned apartment, only to have to deal with a complete stranger roommate who probably has a personality that completely clashes with your own.

But, honestly, I didn't have any idea how bad it could actually be. My new roommate turned out to be a single, thirty-something cat lady who seemed suspicious of me from the second I shook her hand. The first thing she told me was that her mother had just helped her clean the apartment, so I'd better not get it too messy. And to make matters worse, my room didn't even have a door that locked.

I just wanted to get the fuck out of there. I dropped my stuff in my room and left, and called Jacqueline as soon as I got outside to tell her how things were. But when she picked up the phone, I couldn't. I was already drowning in self-doubt, and I didn't want her to hear that in my voice, letting on that I thought I'd made the wrong decision. I lied and told her that everything was going smoothly, then walked to a cigar store and immediately ordered four. I spent the rest of that first afternoon sitting on their couch until they closed, watching television, drinking soda water, and wondering what the hell I'd gotten myself into. And the next two days, I barely left my room. I just paged through the Alinea cookbook over and over again, preparing for my first day and also trying to re-mind myself why I'd sacrificed so many great things in New York to be there.

I started on a Wednesday in the middle of August, and I remember that it was unseasonably mild, almost cool in the morning as I waited for the train underground. But that didn't stop me from sweating bullets. Staging at Alinea had probably been the single most stressful experience of my culinary ca-reer, and I was nervous as hell to begin work there for real.

I quickly found that the key to my success at Alinea would be establishing and sticking to a routine. I needed to be disci-plined in a way that I'd never been about my life before. Every morning, I left my apartment at nine A.M. and took the Red Line train to North and Clybourn. After leaving the subway station, I walked into the Borders on the corner and ordered an egg on a bagel, an iced coffee, and a green Naked Juice. I knew if I didn't start eating breakfast regularly that I wouldn't make it to family meal at four P.M. I also had implemented a four-cigarettes-per-day rule. One when I woke up, one on my way from Borders to Alinea, one at family meal, and one when I got off work. Maybe I thought that if I regulated my personal life, it would somehow give me the discipline I knew I needed at work.

Everything at that point in my life became orderly. Alinea taught me that if things weren't routine, things would quickly become fucked up. For all the oddball, weird shit they did with food, they pretty much functioned like a French kitchen from the 1980s—mimicking their reputations for accepting nothing short of total organization, complete orders and discipline. Pretty quickly, I also found that the extreme order and high standards at Alinea began to affect the way I went about my day-to-day life, so that at all times, I was walking, talking, and acting as if I was at work. If someone took too long in front of me in an aisle at the grocery store, I'd get frustrated and start mouthing off about how they were lazy. It was amazing how quickly the culture of superiority and control seeped into me.

About a week into my tenure at Alinea, I made my first big mistake. One of the garnishes on my station for the pork belly dish was Thai young coconut, which is one of my least favorite ingredients to prep—it's a total bitch to work with, having almost no yield, although their water does make for a powerful hangover tonic. The only workable meat, and I'm talking two ounces tops, sits inside the pointed-top, barrel-bottomed shell—literally just a quarter inch of flesh. The hard part is getting it out intact. I had to clean three to four of these hellish drupes a day. It sounds like nothing, but I had the abrasions on my knuckles for a month after my last day to prove it.

To break down this coconut in the manner that Chef wanted, I had to take a meat cleaver and crack it with the heel of the blade and drain the water from inside. The water had to be preserved, because it would later be used as part of the coconut curry for the same dish. The cracking was insane, involving a loud ruckus completely contrary to the quiet work that would be going on either side of me. Once it was cracked, I had to take a spoon, preferably flatt-ish, with metal that wasn't too thick, and work my way between the fibrous skin and the tender, extremely fragile fruit. As I prepped them, I would so fear breaking the flesh that I would dig the spoon so hard into the shell that my knuckles would constantly be skinned.

When I finally removed the meat, it looked sort of like a flimsy, white bowl that couldn't stand up by itself. After removing the flesh from all four Thai coconuts, I was left with eight pieces. From there I would begin the actual knife work: Cut the coconut into a square, then take that quarter-inch-thick square and fillet it like I was skinning a fish—six times over—so I ended up with about five decent poster-board-thin sheets of coconut. The distinction between paper-thin and poster-board-thin sounds ridiculous, but it was important. After the coconut was "sheeted," I then had to julienne the sheets into rectangles an eighth of an inch wide and one inch long, and then take those rectangles and cut them lengthwise into three equal slices. From there I used offset tweezers to pick up the tiny filaments in three-strand increments while keeping them together. I had two dampened napkins between which I placed the coconut to keep the strands as fresh as possible through service—taste and texturally speaking, that is. When it came time to actually put it on the plate, I had to, in one fluid motion, set one end down on the plate while flipping my tweezers to create a sort of ribbon on the plate. That plate, however, was glass, and coconut is damp, so it's always kind of a one-shot deal.

I'll never forget the night that I ran out of Thai coconut ribbons at nine P.M. during service at Alinea. Not because I didn't prepare enough but because we actually ran out of coconuts to prepare. I had fucked up the plating on too many dishes and had to replace the ribbons that weren't perfect with better-looking ribbons. This led to the possibility that we could run out. My tournant, Nell, was one of the most easy-going cooks at Alinea, but I could see in her eyes what a big deal this could turn out to be. When I told her what was up, she immediately looked at me and just said one word, "Run." So I ran.

As I bolted out the back door I couldn't help but think how ironic this was. I was basically living out a story in the Alinea cookbook about a cook in the same situation. Because of the similarity, Michael Nagrant, a Chicago food critic and a friend of mine, asked me if this was actually true when he heard my story. I guess this is routine for Alinea.

There was a Whole Foods exactly .7 miles away from Alinea, and that was going to have to be my salvation. I ran down Halsted and turned right onto North. I ran so fast that I lost my clogs twice. I got to Whole Foods and ran through the door, scrambling to find anyone who worked there. "Thai coconut, Thai coconut, Thai coconut," I said, ranting like a fucking schizophrenic. I'm pretty sure I scared the shit out of the entire closing staff in the produce section. But Whole Foods was my only hope. If they didn't have Thai coconuts there, I was fucked.

One man pointed toward the specialty booth, and my eyes started darting among the pieces of produce. There was dragon fruit, fresh tamarind pods, and finally, yes, the fucking Thai coconuts. There wasn't even time to catch my breath.

I grabbed the last two coconuts and ran to the cashier. There was no time to make change. I had twenty dollars in my pocket, so I reached down to grab the bunched-up bill and threw it in her general direction, yelling back at her that I was going to lose my job if I didn't leave right that second.

I ran out onto the street, and headed back toward the restaurant. But just as I began to sprint, the bag busted and my two cursed fucking coconuts hit the sidewalk. I turned around, picked them up, and proceeded to make the dash for home plate. And then, just as I was about to reach the door to the restaurant, my stomach started to churn. I was gasping for breath, and a sharp pain was poking through my side. I stopped, panting, and puked everywhere. I don't fucking run. I've been a pack-a-day smoker since I was fifteen, not to mention all the crack and weed smoke on top of it. Still, I had a job to do. I wiped my mouth and got myself together and walked through the back door, calmly handing the coconuts to Nell and then taking my place at the station, stirring the pork belly curry on the induction burner. I was still breathing heavy, noticeably in pain, and Chef Beran came up to me and gave me a little-more-than-a-tap on the chest while smiling and saying, "How those lungs feel, Chef?" And I knew at that moment, I was accepted as a cook at Alinea.

Things were finally starting to settle in. Then, in my third week at Alinea, disaster struck. If the Thai coconut was a test of my resolve as a cook, this was a test of my resolve as a person. And I hate to admit that I didn't fare nearly as well.

I had just finished a shift when I got an urgent phone call from my mother. There had been a drive-by shooting in her

Jacksonville neighborhood. It wasn't the first time—it was a rough neighborhood that had only gotten worse over time. But this time, the house where she lived with her wife and her wife's mother had been hit. Thankfully, everyone was safe, but there were multiple bullet holes in the house. There was damage to the house, and they didn't have much money to deal with that, but more than anything else, they were scared shitless.

The timing couldn't have been worse. I had just gotten into my groove at Alinea, had just started to settle in to Chicago. But I didn't have any choice. I knew I had to fly down to Jacksonville to see my mom, and help out however I could.

I called Alinea and told the reservationist what had happened, and just a few minutes later, Christian Seel, one of the cooks, was on the phone. I explained the circumstances, emphasized how urgent it was, and told him that I would be back at work in two days. He was understanding, wished me a good trip, and said that he would see me in two days.

I remember the phone call vividly, his voice echoing in my ear, me nodding along with the call as I said I would be back. But somehow, I must have known I wouldn't. That I couldn't handle this kind of challenge this early on. I was standing on a street corner in Old Town as I talked to him. And as soon as I hung up the phone, I went to the nearest bar and ordered a beer. I had been completely sober for nine months, by far the longest stretch in my adult life. It had been so long, I didn't even know what to drink. And in less than a minute, it was all over.

I got down to Jacksonville and started drinking that night

with my mother and her wife. She's been off drugs for years, but she still drinks plenty, especially in a situation as stressful as that. I easily joined in, and then started running into old friends in Jacksonville, and because I hadn't learned how to control my impulses—I had just quit completely, cold turkey—I didn't know how to drink in moderation.

Once I'd gotten back on the bottle, it affected my whole way of thinking. I do credit NA with helping me get clean in New York, and I know that I wouldn't have been able to do it without the support of my friends. But there is something about the absolutism of their ethos that, once I slipped, made me rethink everything about my life. I was sure that drinking meant I was immediately going to go back to harder drugs, and that I wasn't going to be able to keep up at Alinea—it was a story we heard over and over again at meetings. You couldn't have just one beer without ruining your whole life.

And so, as two days in Jacksonville turned into three and I hadn't showed back up to work at Alinea, I made a difficult decision. As messages from the chefs started to flood my inbox, I decided I was going to beat them to the punch. Instead of setting myself up for what was sure to be ultimate failure, I drafted and sent my letter of resignation. In retrospect, of course, I wish I'd stuck it out a little longer. I didn't ultimately backslide right away, and I know I still had a lot to learn from working there. But at the time, it felt like I was saving everyone a lot of time and trouble. I tried not to overthink what could have been, so I focused on my feelings of frustration and mentally prepared myself to return to reality.

After four days in Jacksonville, I returned to Chicago

stressed and ashamed. Not only had I just squandered my dream job and my sobriety, but also, with no salary, I didn't know how I was going to pay my rent. If that's how I was feeling on the inside, I certainly didn't project it. I'm not exactly the type to come back with my tail between my legs. Immediately, I did two things. First, I told my roommate that I was going to be late on rent. I didn't think it was that big a deal, since I had given her twelve-hundred dollars—half for the first month's rent, and the other half for a deposit. But if shit had started out badly with my roommate, it certainly hadn't gotten better. She was just a sad fucking lady—mid-thirties with two cats and no job. The men she dated were old as fuck, but that's how she got to go to the most expensive restaurants in Chicago. And I started to guess that her ancient boyfriends were paying her half of the rent.

The other thing I did was order some weed. It didn't seem like a big deal. I was stressed about the job and the rent, and weed always calmed me down. And I had already started drinking again, and given up on Alinea, so I figured I didn't really have anything else to lose.

I was wrong about that. There was something left, or at least, someone. When Jacqueline had agreed to get back together with me after I stole her money and did my stint in Bellevue, she did so on one condition: I would get sober, and stay that way. And the girl was not fucking around. As soon as I slipped up, she was gone, true to her word. I called to tell her what had happened. She hung up on me. A few days later, she flew to Chicago to collect two of her books that I had, and was gone before I even knew she was in town.

With Jacqueline out of the picture, I decided to call an old acquaintance that I had briefly met during my time in New York. Her name was Leigh, and she had lived just around the corner from 6th Street Kitchen. She was smart as fuck—she'd gone to Columbia and had recently moved to the Midwest to start a PhD at the University of Chicago.

A few nights after I told my roommate I would be late on rent, I went to see Leigh. The Bears were playing their season opener against the Detroit Lions, and she invited me over to her apartment in Wicker Park to watch the game. When I showed up with a case of beer and jeans tighter than her own, she laughed at me and called me a hipster, and we settled in for the night. We drank beer, watched the Bears game, and talked about Chicago and New York. I also cooked some crazy dinner for us out of random leftovers in the fridge and some fruit that was about to go bad. If that doesn't impress the ladies, I don't know what does.

I left that night drunk and happy, thinking maybe there was a future for me in Chicago, even though it wasn't turning out as I had planned. What I didn't realize is that my crazy bitch of a roommate had changed the locks on my apartment. I banged on the door for hours, called her over and over again, and finally called the police. But even they were no help. It was her apartment, and I didn't have a lease or anything— legally, I had no rights to get in. And so, again, I was without a place to live, without my cookbooks or a stitch of clothing, except what I had on my back.

I still didn't know many people in Chicago, so in desperation, I went straight back to Leigh's apartment. Not exactly standard procedure after hanging out for one night, but these were extenuating circumstances. Leigh offered to let me stay at her apartment while I looked for a new job and a better place to live. But, of course, after staying with Leigh for about a week, things started to fall into place and we quickly became more than friends. I settled into a totally different lifestyle in Wicker Park from the one I'd just abandoned along with most of my worldly possessions. I was able to convince the cat lady to let me back in one more time to take whatever I could carry, and who knows what she did with all my cookbooks and a bunch of men's clothing, but, hopefully, she felt vindicated somehow. Armed with my knives and my laptop, I convinced myself to make the most of my decision to stay in Chicago.

I spent most of my first week at Leigh's scanning the Internet for jobs, and it wasn't long before the perfect one appeared on Craigslist—Schwa was hiring. I slammed the computer shut and bolted out the door. I ran all the way to Schwa. I told the sous that I had seen the ad on Craigslist and that I had eaten there two months earlier, when Grant Achatz had made a special reservation for me during my stage trip. After two stages, they hired me.

I quickly came to learn that, for such similar restaurants, Schwa and Alinea could not have worked more differently. Alinea worked like clockwork, on military precision. And Schwa seemed to be one miscommunication after another, mostly thanks to the disorganized chef who seemed to rather "fly by the seat of his pants." We wouldn't ever find out till three A.M. at a bar what time we were supposed to come in the next day. For the first week, I would show up about an hour early and get in trouble for it. I recall one day that I came in at eleven A.M., which was what the chef had told me, but for some reason he thought he'd said ten thirty. I was sent home that day as punishment. Two weeks into it, I received a call from the line cook saying that he was going to be late. Immediately, my phone died, so I didn't get the rest of the message, and I came in at my scheduled time. This motherfucker had just assumed I heard him tell me I had to come in early, actually, and wait out front of the restaurant for a snail roe package for the special lunch we were cooking the next day for the hip-hop group Atmosphere. It was just an utter fucking shit show.

I did manage to get fired from Schwa, but it wasn't for any of the usual reasons. It wasn't alcohol or drugs, or even any of the thousands of misunderstandings that seemed to plague the kitchen every day. Instead, it was a stupid-ass skateboard. I hadn't skated since I was a kid, but I'd borrowed one from someone and was amazed at how quickly it got me around the city. What I hadn't counted on was that, just a few weeks into working at Schwa, I broke my ankle. Not usually grounds for losing a job, but it meant that I couldn't easily get around the kitchen. Bad fucking luck.

I was pretty down when I lost the job at Schwa, and seriously considered moving back to New York. It felt like Chicago had been nothing but bad break after bad break—in this case, literally. Things had been going so well in New York, and it seemed like Chicago just made everything go to shit. I was ready to throw in the towel and run back to all the people I'd left behind.

But Chicago did have one thing going for it: Leigh. The night I got fired, she came to Schwa and picked me up. She could see how frustrated I was, and convinced me to get out of the city for a night to think things over. We drove all the way to Milwaukee and spent the night drinking at a random bar and shooting the shit with a guy who I could have sworn was Anthony Bourdain's stunt double.

It wasn't an easy decision, but Leigh had made her case. I hadn't been in Chicago long enough to really see what it had to offer me. There were exciting things happening in food there, and our relationship was going well. If I went back to New York, who knew what would happen? Without much of another plan, I decided to stay in Chicago, at least until it wasn't financially feasible.

I was still worried about my family, but I didn't want to spend the money on a plane ticket, so after making the plan to stay in Chicago, I decided to take a bus down to Jacksonville to check in with them. That was a bad fucking idea—twenty-eight hours of my life that I'll never get back.

I was in Florida for about a day and a half when I got a call from Chicago that seemed too good to be true. It was from the owner of a restaurant called Mado that had received some pretty high praise when under the direction of Rob and Allie Levitt. They had seen my resume and wanted to talk. So I got on the next flight out and the next morning the owner, David Richards, met me at his restaurant, Sweets and Savories, to explain the situation.

According to Richards, Rob and Allie had recently left Mado to open their own butcher shop. That seemed feasible, since Mado was a very meat-heavy restaurant—there was a strong focus on charcuterie on the menu, and they often gave butchering demos. I could hardly believe it when Dave explained that he was looking for someone to take over the reins completely and overhaul the place, which meant total freedom to re-create the menu. Sounded good to me. Finally, carte blanche to do my own food again. It didn't occur to me to look into the situation much further before accepting the job. I was broke, jobless, and just offered my own restaurant. The only problem? I had to hire a staff, redo the menu, change the décor, and open in less than forty-eight hours.

Mado was certainly going to be a challenge, but I was up for it. And when I started, it was awesome. I hired a friend of mine, Emmanuel Cadengo, who had just pulled out of a local culinary school. He suggested some other people I could use to staff my kitchen and I took him up on them, given how quickly I needed to completely change everything about the restaurant, even the paint on the walls and the furniture. At first, things seemed to be going well. I developed a menu and started figuring out where to source the product. I was gaining familiarity with the Chicago purveyors from calling in orders left and right in preparation for our reopening. My staff was maybe a bit underexperienced, but they were for the most part incredibly dedicated and wanted to be there. That's half the battle.

The other half of the battle, unfortunately, as I was about to learn, is to not have an owner who is transferring profits out of your restaurant and into financing a bistro in Wilmette. I first noticed a problem when one of my purveyors stopped selling to me because a check that David Richards had written had bounced. This was week two. Then, all of a sudden, my staff wasn't getting paid. Things went steadily downhill from there. But the final straw was when rumors began circulating that we were operating without proper licensing. I couldn't possibly understand what would compel someone to try to run a restaurant without proper licensing. But, apparently, that becomes a viable option when capital from one restaurant is needed to float the others.

Through no fault of my own I was suddenly front and center in this shambles of a restaurant. All the public heard was that I, once again, quit a cushy job that most people would kill to have. In reality, my staff and I walked out of the restaurant because we did not have fresh food to serve people. Our purveyors were dropping us like used condoms, and my staff weren't getting paid. It was an agonizing decision, but I didn't see any other options. I may not have always made the best decisions, but I do have integrity. And I wasn't about to lead an organization that wasn't even paying its employees. Mado shuttered the night we walked out, never to reopen again.

As much of a disaster as Mado was, though, I can see now that it was an incredibly valuable learning experience. And, in a way, it gave me the confidence that I would need to move forward in Chicago. Though I had cooked at nearly every kind of restaurant in the last several years—from a coffee shop to a shitty Irish pub to a Michelin three-starred palace, I knew now that, not only could I cook, but I could successfully open a restaurant. I needed to pick my business partners more carefully and I needed to cook my own food. But it wasn't just possible, it was probable. And that gave me a dream that, until that point, had been relegated to the back of my brain.

Unfortunately, though, the stress of the situation had brought back my old habits with a vengeance. I had begun using again, and my life was headed toward chaos. And, for the first time, I got a taste of the media spotlight and how vengeful the press can be. I was being called out in papers and on blogs by disgruntled staff members who were rightfully pissed about their last weeks' pay. The anger was misdirected, but someone had to be held accountable, and it wasn't going to be Dave Richards, who had skulked away to his failing restaurant in Wilmette.

I spent the next few months contemplating my next move. I organized a pop-up dinner or two, one of which I didn't even attend on account of my drug habit picking up steam, though my name was used for promotional purposes and the thing was apparently a complete shit show. What's worse is that they lied to the guests about me being there.

That failed pop-up was a particularly low point that year, even though I wasn't even there to witness it. In short, I mostly remember feeling like a worthless piece of shit. Leigh was busy working on her PhD at the University of Chicago, which meant that she was gone a lot and I was alone most of the day. It was also the middle of winter, which is a pretty fucking dismal time to live in Chicago. I had no real desire to leave the house, so I just sat around and did drugs and looked at the bleak weather outside my window. And I knew that this wasn't a good situation—I had moped around long enough. It was time to get serious about finding a new job. I saw an ad for a new restaurant opening in the South Loop of Chicago. They were looking for a chef to do modern takes on American classics. I thought I could take it one step further.

The restaurant was going to be called Tribute, and it was to open in the Essex Inn on Michigan Avenue in the South Loop. It was a cool part of town, just kind of coming into its own, and after answering the ad, I arranged to meet there with Simon Lamb, one of the owners. The meeting went well—he seemed enthusiastic about my ideas and experiences and unfazed by what had happened at Mado—and we arranged meetings for a second and third time with the other two partners involved in the project. After about two weeks of back-and-forth discussions, a date was set for me to do a tasting.

Since the job was for a restaurant that didn't yet exist, there was no sous or other staff to help me with the tasting, so I enlisted the help of a stagiaire I had at Mado named Jacob Sokol. The plan was to do a five-course menu named after cities in America that inspired me, which seemed appropriate, since the whole idea of Tribute was to pay homage to new American classics.

I started with Minneapolis, where I had lived for a few months after touring with Kylesa. I composed a solid soda made from carbonated beet juice. The connection to Minneapolis wasn't obvious, but to me it made sense—all the crust punks in Minneapolis that I used to hang around would spend part of the fall harvesting beets in North Dakota for a decent amount of under-the-table cash.

The second course was inspired by a classic New York brunch, certainly something I was familiar with after five years in the city. It was a cube of brioche stuffed with a banana puree that was spiked with cholula hot sauce, served by the side of a baked egg-and-celeriac dish that I had seen in Fergus Henderson's cookbook *The Whole Beast.*

For the third course, I took Lamb and his partners on a trip back to St. Augustine, Florida, where I'd lived briefly after Savannah. St. Augustine has a large population of Minorcans, and while I was there, I'd learned a little bit about their style of cooking. So I seared red snapper and placed it on top of perfectly tournéed potatoes, carrots, and celery, with clams, and a hearty sauce of datil peppers, clam juice, and tomatoes.

For the main meat course, I thought about the Lowcountry and South Carolina. I confited pork belly in pork fat after curing it in a "wet cure" consisting of mirepoix, mustard seed, celery seed, salt, and sugar. I then seared it and glazed it in a South Carolinian mustard barbecue sauce. I made a sweet potato panna cotta out of sweet potato puree and carrageenan and topped the circular panna cotta with a sheet of green apple gel. The veg part of the course was microplaned brussels sprouts seasoned with apple cider vinegar, fine herbs, and a light aioli to replicate a coleslaw. It was placed in a quenelle next to the pork and panna cotta. The dish was finished with three dots of a beer fluid gel that I had made from a lager and gellant.

I called the last dish "Carnival," and it was a nod to my new Midwestern roots. I was still new to this part of the country and didn't know much about it, but I did know that they had epic state fairs. With that in mind, I made a waffle cone with a cheesecake filling, topped it with a bubble-gum stock that was aerated with lecithin into bubbles, and completed it with pop rocks.

It's safe to say that Simon Lamb and his partners were sufficiently impressed. A few weeks later, I was doing a Mexican-themed pop-up dinner with Emmanuel Cadengo, my sous from Mado. Simon Lamb and one of Tribute's other investors attended the dinner and came equipped with a job offer and the paperwork to prove it. I signed the contracts in the kitchen after we sent out the last course, churros with dulce de leche.

Work began immediately, and while it was intense, it was also fucking exhilarating. If I thought Mado was a lot of work, it was little league compared to this. Within two months, I had to find a staff for a two-hundred-seat restaurant, plus breakfast, lunch, dinner, banquet, and room service menus, open to the public by March 14. There was a lot of money involved in this project, and especially after Mado, it felt like the press was following my every move.

But there were also some serious perks that came with all that work. All of a sudden, I had a $65,000-a-year job. And that's not all: One of the investors found me a full-floor, two-bedroom penthouse loft in the South Loop equipped with a professional kitchen and a stage in the living room. I was told by the owner of the loft that it used to be R. Kelly's old recording studio. No shit.

I had money, a swank pad, and things were finally looking back on track in my life. Yet again, I couldn't believe the way my luck seemed to turn around at the flick of a switch. Just a few months ago, I was locked out of my apartment with no money, no job, and no clothes except the ones I had on my back. Now, shit had officially turned around.

At the restaurant, I started by hiring my sous chefs. We interviewed fourteen chefs, brought six back to do tastings, and hired three. With them on board, we began menu testing and weekly planning in preparation of opening. I loved the idea of it all—new American classics, with freedom to play with dishes and make them our own. We worked on renditions of dishes like matzoh ball soup, Oregon Trail concepts like coffee and beans served in a can on top of a Sterno, and even apple and cheddar Pop-Tarts with bacon-fat frosting. I obsessed over the menus, going back time and time again to make sure they were perfect, innovative, fresh, and, most important, delicious. After all the bullshit I had gone through in Chicago, after every stroke of bad luck, Tribute was how I was going to say to the world: "Fuck you, look at me now."

But then things started going downhill. The opening kept getting pushed back, largely owing to complications with the unions. A March 14 opening was pushed all the way back to May, and things started to fall apart. We had enough to pay the lead sous chefs, but I was behind about a month in paying the two junior sous. We had already hired the line cooks, but since the opening was delayed, we couldn't pay them yet, and some had already put in their notice, leaving us back at square one.

But at the same time, my fall from sobriety was growing more and more dangerous, spinning completely out of control. I had started out with just alcohol, moved on to pot, then got back into cocaine, and finally, for the first time since Nora and DC, I started smoking crack again. I thought I could balance things, that I was experienced now and on top of my shit, not just some dumb kid anymore. And for the first month, I did manage it well.

As my drug use increased, Leigh also began having second thoughts about things. I'd moved out of her apartment when I got the new place near Tribute, but the more I used, the less she wanted to spend any time with me at all. I wanted to be with her and tried to curb my crack consumption, but I couldn't, and she couldn't stick around. She dumped me, and my life started to spiral out of control.

One morning in late April, I shaved my head into a Mohawk and went to a friends and family event at the not-yet-opened Union Sushi and Barbecue Bar. I got wickedly drunk and left with a craving for cocaine like I'd never had before. In a frenzy, I called my drug dealer, and when he left, I held about six hundred dollars of crack in my hand. I went back to my loft, abandoned all of my responsibilities at Tribute, and began a four-day binge of smoking and fucking. It all ended with me meeting a girl named Rachael for dinner at Blue 13.

Unbelievably, I met Rachael over Twitter. I was high and fucking around on the Internet and saw some things she had posted—this girl was funny as hell, and cute, too, from her pictures. We started writing back and forth and I sent her a direct message to hang out. I'm not sure why, but she agreed to meet me a few days later at Blue 13, a now-closed restaurant that I'd been meaning to check out. It was clear from the beginning that we had chemistry, and after beef tartare and numerous whiskeys, we headed back to her place and hung out for a bit in her bed, talking, kissing, whatever. It was one of the best first dates of my life.

I saw her again a few days later, and decided to grab a couple of grams of coke on the way to her house. Rachael wasn't into drugs at all—I came to find out that she didn't even drink much, contrary to all those whiskeys. But she didn't seem to mind me doing it there. I stayed all night, wired on coke, hanging out with her. She would fall asleep for about twenty minutes and I'd get up to do a line of cocaine, and when I returned, she'd be ready for another go. This went on all night until the time she had to get up to leave for work. She told me to stay put and I agreed. I ended up "staying put" for four days.

At this point, I'd basically been MIA from Tribute for a few weeks, which was a disaster, especially as we were getting ready to open. I'd stopped answering my phone, and ignored the computer, knowing that whatever was waiting for me couldn't possibly be good.

On the fourth day at Rachael's apartment, I finally checked my e-mail, and there it was, from Simon Lamb. After my first binge, he had told me I would be suspended for two weeks to go to rehab. Now, he wrote, I had been terminated. I was surprised, actually, at how humane he was. The situation was shitty, but he actually seemed to care about me getting help. But, I realized as I saw the e-mail, this wasn't like getting fired from any other job. The press had been following the opening closely, and they would be on this faster than I could even imagine. I knew I had to get my shit in gear, and quickly, and started by writing back to Simon asking if they could keep it under wraps from the press until I found a suitable treatment program. He responded that he would try.

Ten minutes later, I received a direct message on Twitter from a local food critic asking me what had happened at Tribute. It wasn't anybody's fault, but the news had broken, and I had to face the music. Tribute didn't release any of the actual reasons but said they had replaced me with the sous I hired, Lawrence Letrero. They would eventually open on July 7, months later than planned. I knew the late opening was because of the same union disputes I had dealt with in the spring, but, not surprisingly, most of the food blogs blamed it on me.

With the news all over the Internet, Rachael quickly found out what had happened and told me that if I were to go into treatment, I could stay with her and take some time off from everything to focus on my sobriety. I was thankful for her kindness, and quickly found myself falling for her. With her support, I thought, maybe I could do this all over again, and this time in a real way.

But first, I had to face rehab. And this time, I wasn't just some anonymous asshole heading to a state facility on Staten Island. The press surrounding what had happened at Tribute had gotten to be so big around Chicago that a reporter for the *Chicago Tribune* asked if he could trail me as I went to rehab. He wanted to do a big profile on me and my rise and subsequent demise in the Chicago food world. I went back and forth about the article—it's humiliating, of course, to have all of your demons out there in the open. But I've always been honest, if nothing else. And I did figure that this would at least tell some of my side of the story, too.

At the same time, I had to figure out what I was going to do professionally. I knew that at that point, in Chicago at least, I was totally fucking unhirable. I had actually managed to sober up, partially thanks to the couple of days in rehab, partially thanks to NA meetings, partially thanks to Rachael, and partially because I just knew it was about time. But, as far as the public knew, I was a total loose cannon.

Maybe, I figured, it was time to start my own brand. It was time to stop working for other people and it was time to take control of my own destiny. And that would look different from anything anyone else was doing. I was going to launch the "anti-restaurant," one without the traditional confines of one location, one menu, one chef. It was something I hoped would start in Chicago but build around the country. I wanted it to be bigger than this one city, bigger than just me, even. Now all I needed was a name.

I debated on a name for the new project for weeks. I wanted something comforting at first, something that conjured up the feelings of "home." This was particularly important to me, because in many ways, I felt I'd never really had one. I'd probably moved hundreds of times in my life, starting from when I was a little kid, so home was never about a pile of bricks. More than anything, just as I hoped it would be in my new project, home was about the food. I thought about calling it Abode, Eason's (my mother's maiden name), Endure, and Sojurn. But finally, it was Rachael who came up with the winner. I shouldn't have been surprised—she was creative and incredibly bright, so she knew how to capture what was really important about a concept. She suggested that I was overlooking what this new project was really about. Not feeling at home, but rather, doing something new, something important. She suggested Crux, which meant, poignantly, the most important part.

I was immediately sold. Crux, fucking Crux. It was genius. It embodied exactly what I wanted people to know about the project. And it just sounded strong. Powerful. Exciting. I figured that the best way to introduce this concept was with one huge debut pop-up dinner—ten courses, all totally mind-blowing. And I wanted to donate all the profits to charity, an addiction recovery group.

To help me pull it off, I brought in some of my most trusted comrades—I enlisted Emmanuel Cadongo, who had been with me since Mado, Jaimee from 6th Street back in New York, and a new kid, Kevin McMullen, who had been working for Andrew Brochu at Kith & Kin. We sold out the first dinner, which was held on the roof of a high-rise building in the South Loop, in forty-eight hours.

The first dinner went well, and, more important, it attracted a whole lot of attention. Some was good, some less so, but people were talking about us and talking about this new way of cooking. A writer from a men's magazine even came and camped out for a few days, while we planned and cooked for that meal, to do a big profile that came out a few months later.

Looking back on the dinner, though, it almost seems funny. I thought what we were doing then was revolutionary. But it wasn't, at least not compared to what we're doing now. But I guess that's what I always hoped for Crux—something constantly changing, always on the cutting edge.

The next year seemed to fly by, with a new project always around the corner. In seven months, Crux put on fifteen different dinners. Some were huge, and some were very small. I never knew who was going to be interested in partnering with us, who was going to have an idea that pushed us in another direction. I managed to stay afloat mostly doing that, though I took a job briefly at an Italian restaurant called Pensiero in Evanston to pay some bills. I knew I wasn't entirely done with restaurant cooking for the rest of my life, but the contrast between churning out someone else's dishes and creating my own entirely new concept was vast, and I found I couldn't wait to get back to Crux.

My personal life, also, was a bit of a roller coaster. After rehab, I officially moved in with Rachael, and she became my partner in life and also the driving force behind the project. I was excited to put down roots and see what life had in store for us. But after the last nine months of sobriety in Chicago, I started to think differently about the ways I wanted to live my life. I certainly wasn't planning on ever going back to the way I had been. But I also knew that I was a different person, and had different ideas of what it meant to be in control. Unfortunately, though, Rachael had seen me at my worst, and she wasn't willing to stick around to see how my new plan would manifest itself. When I took a new stance on sobriety, our relationship came to a halt.

Near the end of Crux in Chicago, I began to drink again. This is important for me to say because it's one thing I know that people have been unclear about. I was forced to look back on what had happened on my twenty-fifth birthday in NYC, the day when I woke up with no will to drink or do drugs any longer. This was the opposite. I woke up with a choice. It was either repeat the same pattern that had ruined my life many times over—the pattern of being clean so long and building up this suppressed urge to do anything and everything I could to get fucked, often leading to the collapse of everything positive around me. Or I could simply grow the fuck up. I had spent the past five years being told by "the program" that, for addicts like me, it was all or nothing. I knew I couldn't be a productive member of society if I was smoking crack, but I also knew that every impulse didn't have to be a gateway to smoking crack.

I know that when I'm told I can't do something, it makes me want to do it more. I went through numerous long stints of not touching any substance other than nicotine and caffeine only to have this built-up, deviant repression go into overdrive leading to binge excess. The thought of normalcy intrigued me. I can't stand the thought of not being able to toast my wife at my wedding, or drink a single-barrel bourbon after dinner at a nice restaurant. Normalcy was something I never thought I could obtain, but I realized that that's what I wanted, even more than I wanted sobriety.

So I decided to take control of my addiction. I decided that if I couldn't maintain a productive life for fear of having a drink, it wasn't a life worth living. I gave up my sobriety at nine months, again, and in the process lost Rachael. I gained something much more powerful, though. I gained acceptance of my problem. I gained insight, and from insight, wisdom was acquired. I knew I had to leave. I had taken everything I could from Chicago, and now it was time to move on. But I didn't want to do it alone. So I went back to the only person in my life other than my mother who, I knew, knew the real me. Leigh.

I called Leigh to tell her what was going on in my life and that I wanted to leave Chicago. I had a few more dinners scheduled that I had to be present at, but after that, the possibilities seemed endless. Leigh was living in a spot in the Ravenswood neighborhood of Chicago, and happened to have a spare room. We weren't getting back together, but we both knew we loved each other. At this point, it wasn't romantic love but something almost more important. She felt like family. I filled her in on everything I was doing with Crux and told her it was time to take it on the road. And, it turned out, she was game to join me. I moved into the spare room, and we prepared to go on the adventure of a lifetime.

CHAPTER NINE

It's hard to know how to pack up an apartment when you have no idea where you're going, but that's just what Leigh and I did at the end of February 2012. It didn't take very long—most of the furniture belonged to the owner, so we threw our clothes and basic necessities into the car, the rest of the stuff in storage, and left a little pile of homeless kitchen stuff for the next tenants. For all the baggage it felt like Chicago had piled on me, in terms of physical items, we were pretty much home free.

Next, we had to figure out a plan. All we knew was that we had to get the hell out of Dodge, mostly for my own sanity. There were too many memories in Chicago, too many toxic forces bringing us down. We had no reason to stay, and an entire country stretched out before us. I have to say, it was one of the most liberating fucking feelings I've ever had.

It was definitely an unconventional situation, moving

back in with my ex-girlfriend. But I guess I'm not much for convention anyway. The status of our relationship wasn't exactly defined—we weren't together, but who knew what the future would hold, especially since we were about to move across the country together. Plus, we'd just added a new member to our weird little family—a pit bull we'd adopted from The Anti-Cruelty Society downtown. In homage to my eye-awakening birthday dinner a few years earlier, we named him Wylie Dufresne.

I've never been a big fan of California, so that was out, even though the weather would have been a welcome change from the dreary gray skies of Chicago in late February. So, at first we looked in the South. Leigh was pretty keen on trying our luck in Georgia or New Orleans, but I had history in the South, and when I thought about it, both somehow seemed more depressing than staying in Chicago.

I tried to convince Leigh that we should spend the money we had in the bank account on camping gear and hike the Appalachian Trail. It was almost March, which would have been the time that many start the northbound hike from Georgia to Maine. Even though she'd get to spend more than enough time in the South, she didn't love the idea, so it was shelved on account of its being too cold even in Georgia to be sleeping outside. Plus, we weren't really familiar with Wylie's behavior yet, so taking him straight from kennel to Cujo may have been a bit of a stretch.

We both agreed we needed to be near water. After paging through cheap rental cottages, we finally settled on a place called the Dolphin Den in Ogunquit, Maine. The logic behind the move was simple: We'd move to an organic agriculture mecca and find a farm that would take us both on as apprentices. It was something that interested both of us, and it was also forward thinking. We'd been talking recently about the feasibility of running a destination restaurant on a farm, likely on a plot of land outside of Chicago. We had our mission statement all mapped out. Over 90 percent of what we'd serve would come directly from our farm (which we'd run ourselves), and the rest would be sourced from other local farmers and operations. Leigh, in particular, wanted practice—she hoped to be able to manage and enjoy the farm while I focused primarily on the restaurant.

The idea of farming, gardening, and living off the land was philosophically appealing to both of us, but also had sentimental appeal. Leigh had spent many of her childhood weekends on her grandparents' farm, and savored the memories of working alongside them and eating the fruits of her labor.

I started to realize that for me, too, the appeal of farming probably came from a man with whom I had more in common than I had ever imagined—my grandfather Thomas Eason. He, like me, never much knew his real father, a Cherokee who was shipped off to World War I. He survived the war and became a traveling salesman when he came home but never returned from his first trip. Some thought he'd been murdered, others thought suicide, but either way, we never heard much about him at the holiday dinner table. My grandfather's mother remarried, though, to a tobacco farmer from North Carolina, and that's where my grandfather was raised, on a farm in the deep Deep South.

Like me, my grandfather was quite the adrenaline junkie. Between 1941 and 1966, he was a test pilot for the navy, including during World War II when the States were using a small, isolated volcanic island called Ascension Island as an airfield named Wideawake. There was an old saying that goes, "If you land on Ascension, your wife gets your pension." My grandfather was one of the first, and lived to tell the tale.

He went on to fly planes for the navy in Korea and Vietnam, where apparently he learned to drink and drug as well. I heard plenty of stories about his drinking when I was growing up. But by the time I was born, he had put down the bottle and was married to a woman named Dottie, who wasn't my grandmother.

All that aside, the Grandaddy Eason I knew was no military man. Instead of telling me war stories, when we would make the drive from Jacksonville, Florida, to Pell City, Alabama, he would talk to me about tomatoes or apples. The man had the greenest thumb of anyone I've ever seen. He lived on a hill directly on a lake, and I loved to run down it and jump in the lake, then make up games about how to get back to my grandfather by climbing "the most biggest and powerful mountain in the universe." I would sometimes be rewarded with a sweet, bold Sungold tomato. I still have an affinity with Sungolds. With every bite, I see my grandfather on his knees, in his straw hat, plucking the weeds by their roots from the beds.

My grandfather also had a downright obsession with ice cream. He was a skinny dude—probably no more than five feet eight inches tall and a hundred and forty pounds, tops. I sat there and watched that man eat a half gallon of ice cream every single night we would visit. I've been told that he did this his entire adult life, once he stopped drinking. Hey, we all trade it in for something. When my grandfather wasn't covered in red clay soil, or eating enough ice cream to stop an elephant from shitting for a solid month, he got his rocks off by scaring the shit out of me.

He had a comb-over, which I didn't know about until I was maybe nine years old. I'm talking like half of his head was about twelve inches of hair and the other half was bald to the skin, which he loved to use to scare me. He would collect Halloween automatons and, as I would be getting ready for bed, he would break them out and talk in a Vincent Price–like voice while howling at the full moon and pushing the buttons on the animated werewolf and zombie figurines. I would already be scared by the time I hit the sack, but it wouldn't end there. He would creep up and down the halls in the middle of the night and when I would wake up and peek out the door, he would be standing there, dressed in the male equivalent of a nightgown, glaring, with a creepy fucking smile and his comb-over hanging to the side, and would let out the most frightening maniacal laugh you've ever heard. I fucking loved that man.

My family buried my granddaddy Thomas when I was eighteen years old, fittingly, right around Halloween. I remember getting the news while I was rehearsing with my Misfits cover band, 138, and we were just getting ready for the annual Halloween show. And the next day, I was on the road with my mother. We shared a pint of whiskey at his funeral, and didn't say much, but I think his death brought us closer. We were all each other had now.

I couldn't help but think how much it would make my granddaddy smile to think of me heading out to work on a farm. I know he'd be proud of all that I'd accomplished, but also, that he'd want me to put down the gels and foams and all that bullshit for a little while, and focus on food grown right there in the ground. Because, when it came right down to it, what could be more perfect than a ripe Sungold tomato, picked with one's own hands?

The next day, we packed two bags of clothes into the trusty MINI Cooper, along with Wylie and our dreams, and set off for Maine. We were covered for housing for a month and figured it couldn't possibly take longer than that to find a good place to land. On our way, we also planned a slight detour. I had recently been in touch with a chef named Kevin Sousa, who was working in Pittsburgh and who seemed to share with me some qualities and ideologies. Western Pennsylvania was on our way anyway, so I figured it was worth making a stop and checking out his restaurant.

It's pretty safe to say that we ate our way through Pittsburgh. First, we stopped at Sousa's barbecue restaurant, Union Pig and Chicken, which serves some of the best fried chicken I've ever eaten, not to mention brisket, ribs, and all the appropriate sides. After a quick nap, we made our way back into Pittsburgh's Garfield neighborhood to see what his other restaurant, Salt of the Earth, had to offer. The food was great, but the most memorable part of the meal was the warmth and hospitality that we felt as we sat at the bar lining the open kitchen. We chatted with the cooks about food, music, and Pittsburgh while sampling pretty much the entire menu and a few extra plates they threw our way. One dish, made by Chad Townsend, the chef de cuisine, in particular stood out—blood-orange segments, red onion, cress, and lardo. It was perfection.

I left Pittsburgh with a deeper appreciation for the city, as well as a few new like-minded acquaintances. All in all, it felt like we had made the right decision to see what was there for us outside of Chicago. With that, we made our way across the massively wide state of Pennsylvania and up the East Coast.

I had never been to Maine before, and as we started to creep up the coast, I was getting more and more excited. Leigh had visited once as a kid, but all she remembered about Maine were tide pools, whale watching over frigid water (they were out on the boat four hours and saw "one silly humpback") and, of course, the lobster. Ogunquit is a town not too far from the New Hampshire border, but the difference, in vibe especially, between the two states is striking. I would soon grow so accustomed to Maine's quirks that I'd begin to emulate them. But at the time, it seemed as if we had stepped onto the set of a movie about a small-town lobsterman in the early 1900s.

When we pulled up to the Dolphin Den, just a block from the Atlantic Ocean, we were greeted by Rick, the friendly, slightly overbearing owner. We were able to afford the little cottage only because—and Rick pointed this out numerous times—it was the off-season, only early March. In just two short months, it would become a desirable getaway for gay and lesbian couples. After a quick tour, we excused ourselves from Rick and promptly fell asleep, waking up just in time to walk Wylie down to the beach and catch the sunset.

And that's kind of how life went for the next month. We didn't spend time with many people, apart from our neighbor Mary, who made it very clear that she liked Wylie more than she liked us. And we were broke. It seemed unbelievable, but over the course of our first month in Maine, we blew through all the money we both had, and had a hefty amount on the credit card. We kept ourselves sane by visiting Portland (the only sizable city within eighty miles of Ogunquit) and playing massive amounts of video games. I decompressed by smoking pot sometimes, and Leigh took daily walks out to the ocean to sit on the rocks.

Sometimes at night, we wandered over to the local gay bar. I wouldn't say we were regulars, but you could say that all the regulars knew us. There isn't a whole lot to do in these towns until early summer when restaurants and other attractions begin to open for the season, so it seems all the locals develop a bit of alcoholism waiting for May. One such local was a flamboyant black man named Tony. Tony had been in the military, fought in a war, lost a limb, and then came screaming out of the closet. He felt he was making up for decades of lost time in a repressive community by packing a whole lot of sass and drunken debauchery into his forties.

Tony loved Leigh and, as a result, pretended to despise me. Sometimes he was extremely convincing, shouting at me over karaoke music about being a tease or too aloof one minute, then performing a duet of some Journey ballad the next.

He probably felt protective of the one young straight girl in town, but I guess we'll never know for sure since he was never sober enough to express this. And at least he was entertaining.

Though picturesque and serene, life in Ogunquit quickly started to feel somewhat like a gilded birdcage. I felt like a dick, complaining about living, with no real obligations to anyone, a block from the Atlantic Ocean in Maine, but it wasn't always ideal. Most of the local businesses were closed, and because we lived in a studio cottage equipped only with a mini fridge and a microwave as a kitchen, we ended up eating a lot of fast food, and subpar fried seafood at the year-round clam shacks. I would have thought that being a hundred feet from the ocean, more places would serve fresh seafood that didn't come covered in batter and grease.

One place that did take advantage of its proximity to the water was J's Oyster in Portland, a little hole-in-the-wall nestled on the docks between lobster pounds and fish markets. Whenever I went there, I got the same thing: a seafood sampler and a large bucket of steamers. The seafood sampler, which was cheap as hell, had the usual suspects: lobster, crab, shrimp, and raw oysters, but also two gigantic raw scallops. I'd slice through them with a little plastic prong, the same kind that comes with oysters, and they'd melt in my mouth like butter. I ordered my first bucket of steamers as a touristy, novelty thing. I used to fucking love Anthony Bourdain's show, *No Reservations*, and when I thought of Maine, I always pictured the episode of him chowing down on a bucket of steamers. I think I was attached to the idea of the steamers more than the actual experience. They aren't terrible, but even when you become a veteran cleaner of the things, you still always manage to get that little bit of grit with your clam. That said, I ordered them every time I went to J's.

It was also in Portland that the urge to get another tattoo came over me. I'd mostly had the same shitty tattoos covering my body since I was a teenager, and wanted to cover them up with something a little more meaningful and mature. I couldn't think of anything better than fruits and vegetables—earthy, beautiful, and edible.

It took awhile to find the right tattoo shop, largely due to some confusion over my ID, but finally, after walking up and down the streets of Portland, I happened upon a small shop on the second floor of a narrow building. The first thing I noticed was how clean the place was. It seemed like everything—the furniture, equipment, even the floors—was glossy and new. I knew after exchanging a few words with the tattoo artist that this was the man for me.

John Biswell and I had a great conversation about my thoughts on the sleeve. He seemed genuinely excited about the vegetable theme and starting showing me books and catalogues he had in his shop with really great-looking pictures of fruit and veg. I left there with an appointment on the books for two weeks later, wondering how I'd explain my need for a massive amount of money before we'd even secured our farm stay. Over the next few days, I was in contact with Biswell predominantly about the sleeve he was working on for me. However, one morning, he told me we had to come in to meet a friend of his who was getting some work done at the shop. He figured we'd hit it off since we were both in the industry. I have my doubts about categorically lumping people into the friends group simply because they happen to spend sixty hours of their week doing the same shit as each other. It's pretty obvious from my experience that it doesn't always turn out so well. I was really into Biswell, though, so I figured I'd give this guy a shot.

When we got to the shop that afternoon, it turned out Biswell's instincts were right on. He introduced me to Josh Potocki, who was just a bit older than I and owned and worked the line at a bagel place called 158 Pickett Street Café. He was completely relaxed and friendly right off the bat. I was starting to get the sense that everyone in Maine fit that description. Josh had grown up in the middle of nowhere Pennsylvania and had come to Maine on a whim for a vacation twelve years earlier and never left. I would soon find out that his cheerful and laid-back attitude reflected a Zen philosophy of life but also an incredible ability to separate himself from busting his ass every day running his own restaurant.

Though we'd grown to have some interesting times in southern Maine, we were still focused on and excited about the next step of our journey—the farm apprenticeship. When we weren't exploring Portland and eating fried seafood at shacks on the roadside of Highway 1, we dedicated most of our free time to finding one. We applied to a few, and actually heard back from all the farms that interested us, but we were especially excited when we got a call from an organic vegetable farm in Etna, Maine. It's certified organic by the Maine Organic Farmers and Gardeners Associations (MOFGA), one of the oldest and most established organic associations in the country, which helps foster a strong sense of community and a supportive infrastructure. Once we found out that the veg farm had a partnership with a nearby livestock farm, we were pretty much sold.

Things had gotten pretty weird at the Dolphin Den, so we decided to leave a week before our move and do some camping in the wilderness of Maine. I still hadn't seen a moose, and from all the talk at the tattoo shop about encounters with moose, not to mention the fact that Maine has a moose-hunting lottery in place, I figured I was bound to see one if I got far enough into the woods. We still didn't know all that much about rural Maine, so when we settled on a camping spot near Belfast, we didn't realize that we weren't headed into the woods, but rather, toward the coast. It made for very picturesque camping. The campground I had booked for us was right on the water and our site looked out over Sears Island.

Because it was still too early in the season for any touristy things to be open for business, we pretty much roughed it without the usual trimmings of a leisurely camping trip. We couldn't find any kayak or canoe rentals, most restaurants were still closed, even the whale-watching boats hadn't started their tours. So we froze our asses off the first night in the cheap tent I picked up at Walmart on the drive up. Not really taking into account the fact it was the beginning of April and we were almost in fucking Canada, I may have underestimated the need for blankets or sleeping bags. The car was so full, we barely had room for the dog, so we decided on cheap fleece blankets, hoping to survive another night in the tent.

We were underprepared in general for the type of week we had in store—living in the woods and cooking all our food over a fire pit—so we headed into Belfast to stock up at a local chain store that carries everything from clogs to note cards and kitchen equipment. We headed back to the campsite fully stocked with everything needed to brave a few more nights in the great outdoors. My intent was to try to live completely off foraged food from the area. Nature had other plans: Spring had not yet arrived in Maine, restricting our foraging in the area to plants that required a lot of doctoring to actually be enjoyable (and even edible), so we decided to forgo the natural living and ditched the weeds and reeds and bought some hot dogs and Chef Boyardee.

We were out there for four days when finally, a day early, I decided I needed a shower more than I needed to commune with nature. I was cold, smelled like a hippie, and, frankly, was starting to miss the Internet. So we found a motel and treated ourselves to two horrendously overcooked lobsters. When in Maine, right? We packed up the next morning and headed to the farm we would call home for the next four months.

We got to the livestock farm in the middle of the afternoon, rested and ready to begin our new adventure. As we made our way up the driveway, we passed a small vegetable garden with the beginnings of what would become an impressive six rows of spring garlic. Across the driveway were five pens housing about half of the 250 hogs they raised as free-range as possible with animals as curious and adventurous as pigs. No one was home, but we found the door unlocked and a note that said we should feel free to unpack and get situated. The minute I walked into the kitchen, I saw the remains of a home-cooked meal, and I knew we had made the right decision. After unpacking the overstuffed car, we walked around the farm and met the horses, chickens, pigs, and cows that became our roommates that day.

I'd soon come to learn that Heidi, the owner and operator, was famous for her whirlwind lunches, which she'd eat as she was walking out the door on the way to the barn to take care of a fence that needed mending or a farrowing sow. Dinner was another story entirely. We'd gotten a little taste of what dinner would be like earlier in the month, when we'd come up to visit the farm for an afternoon. We hadn't planned on staying for dinner, but when Cleetus, the organic vegetable farmer, took us over to see the fields, it seemed to make sense. The dinner Heidi made for us was incredibly simple and plentiful. We had roasted chicken thighs with beets and greens, and homemade bread with cheese from a local farm. Everything that was served (minus the cheese) had come from one of their farms. Since nothing was even in the ground yet at Cleetus's, the vegetables had come from last year's harvest via the freezer. Although the dinner was essentially functioning as our interview, I remember the conversation being easy and comical. As the family and Cleetus joked about farm-related concepts that Leigh and I couldn't even begin to comprehend at that point, we realized that the family was vetting our personalities more than our nonexistent agricultural skills. After hearing amusing stories about the successes and obstacles faced by neighboring families and farmers, we began to really feel comfortable with the idea of embarking on the incredible learning process ahead. I was stuffed after our meal but soon came to understand that that's what life was like on the farm—Heidi's nine-year-old son, James, had eaten twice as much as I had.

I can't help but laugh, thinking of us unloading the car on the first day—the first things we took out were a TV and PlayStation, which we'd barely touch over the course of the next four months. I was so used to cities and suburbs that I didn't realize what family life could be like without always being attached to electronics. Heidi's daughter, Wendy, was an avid reader. She loved reading lengthy novels (probably meant for kids a couple of years older than her) starring wizards, dwarves, and elves. James, on the other hand, was outside, rain or shine. All across the farm, he had created labyrinthine playgrounds for his trucks. They were both extremely creative kids. It was still comforting to my plugged-in brain to know that we had our technological outlets, but also pretty cool to see a family play outside and read for fun, without relying on all the rest of that shit.

The next morning, we woke up around six and got ready for our first day as farm apprentices. We hadn't yet gotten into any sort of rhythm, and basically had no idea what the fuck we were doing, so we both bumbled around awkwardly on Heidi's farm, asking at each turn how many buckets one group got versus another. We would soon be so in the zone that we could knock out chores, half asleep, in thirty minutes. Though both of us got a lot fitter and stronger during the months we were there, we still couldn't hold a candle to Heidi at chores. She'd grab four ten-gallon buckets in her hands and easily trek across the farm without skipping a beat.

Over the next couple of days, we acclimated to our new schedule and slowly started to learn the ropes of the farm. I remember, in particular, the first time we took a trip to the butcher. It was a two-hour trek each way, with most of it driven down small country roads. Upon finally arriving at what seemed to be someone's home, we were greeted by Arnold and his staff, all wearing butchers' aprons and hairnets. Country music was playing throughout the facility, and some of his employees looked like they weren't even of legal age to drink. Then we unloaded the trailer of "feeder" hogs to be tunneled into pens where they would wait their turn to receive the "kill shot" for which Heidi would shell out twenty dollars apiece. They would not be butchered until our next drop-off.

We picked up three hundred pounds of pork cuts and sausages and rode home to unload it into the freezers in the shop. The stock had been slightly low since we arrived, but now they were filling up with three styles of ribs, chops, butt and shoulder roasts, and six varieties of sausages. It was the trip to the butcher that really illustrated what we were working toward. It had been informative to learn about feeding and housing the animals we were raising, but it was truly rewarding to see that process to its end, and help stock up the shop with the animals we had seen Heidi haul out a few days prior. That night we feasted on pork and enjoyed the fruits of our fledgling labor. Exhausted from the first week of real farmwork, we passed out right after dinner, at the same time as the nine-year-old children.

Soon we were starting to get the hang of things. We were told that, in the farming community, boring is good. All I can say is, there was nothing boring about what we were doing. We were learning new things with every task we were asked to accomplish. Early one morning, we were summoned to assist in our first farrowing. Groggy and tired, we made our way out to the cold, damp barn to watch as a sow birthed fourteen piglets.

I had never seen an animal give birth before, and found myself very moved by the process. It speaks to the high-functioning way of the universe somehow, that there is an instinctual system in place in nature that allows for new members of a species to be born without human help. Hogs have large litters because a large number of newborns are crushed by the mother accidentally or born with their air passages blocked. The sow makes herself a nest a few days before she farrows and, if she's in a pen with other hogs, separates herself from the herd. When it comes time for the birth, the piglets that emerge from the womb go from tiny, sticky, disoriented messes to dry, pristine creatures that develop the ability, within minutes, to hobble out of the way of their siblings coming down the birth canal. The piglets then instinctively find their way to a nipple. The suckling helps the mother's birthing process by releasing hormones that signal for better contractions to help speed the remaining piglets along.

Being a part of the natural birthing process is an awe-inspiring thing, but it can also be valuable to remember, in dire circumstances, the power of human help, too. Sometimes, if a piglet has been "stuck" inside its mother for too long, the restriction of oxygen would all but guarantee that, by the time the newborn came into the world, it would have little to no chance of survival. It might show slight signs of life, but without help, it would soon stop breathing. What's amazing is that it doesn't take much to revive these guys. When they come out, often they'll need their airway cleared of the mucuslike stuff that gets trapped in their mouths and throats. Then it's just a matter of laying them on their side and rubbing them vigorously to jump-start their systems.

During our first farrowing, we watched Heidi revive one such piglet after nearly a half hour of effort. She named the piglet Pathetisad as a reflection of her expectations of its chance at survival. She later revealed to us that had it not been our first farrowing, she probably would have thrown in the towel after five minutes. By the time we left the farm, a few of Pathetisad's siblings had met untimely ends. Some were crushed inadvertently by their mother; some developed illnesses. Despite Pathetisad's rocky start, he was still kicking months later when it came time to sell the piglets. Farming livestock is, in a sense, very close to playing God. In the wild, half of the piglets wouldn't survive the birth, much less the development to adolescence. Looking back, it makes me think about natural selection and the survival-of-the-fittest mentality—that would be "organic." But, when you see a piglet lying on its side and gasping for air, you don't think twice about inserting your fingers into its throat to remove whatever it is that's about to take its life.

With a farrowing under our belts, and the weather starting to warm up, it seemed that things were really beginning to take shape. We started to develop routines on the livestock farm, and even began to understand that "boring" really was better. There were obviously some hiccups. Every once in a while the electric fencing would get buried, and the pigs would escape. There's nothing more comical and frustrating than being out in the freezing cold trying to herd a bunch of hogs back into their pens. On one such occasion, it took the entire family (including the two nine-year-olds) to corner a rogue boar and get him back into his stall. He was being held alone in a stall temporarily, but boars are known to break out of solitary confinement to chase tail. I could understand that. A man wants what a man wants.

Things were picking up steam on Cleetus's vegetable farm, too, where we had started to plant seedlings in trays. They are allowed time to sprout indoors (in this case in his kitchen under heat lamps) and then are taken to a hoop house, where they sit and become hardier until they are ready to be transplanted. Weeks later, you get the visual gratification of the hours you spent hunched over hundreds of trays, dropping one or two seeds into the individual cells. When that first bit of green pokes out from the soil, there's a sense of profound accomplishment, and also relief—all of that nurturing had not been for nothing.

Every day was fulfilling in some way on the farm. It was nice to feel so worn out after a day's work that the only energy I had left was just enough to climb the stairs to the bedroom. Our days were long and full of new experiences, but as weeks turned into months, I found myself looking forward to the weekend farmers' markets when I went into Portland with Heidi to sell meat. Life on the farm was purifying and rewarding, but the group of friends we had in Portland were a constant reminder of my true calling, which will soon involve a farm but must always involve a kitchen.

As apprentices, we were asked to cook for the family once a week, and of course I always looked forward to those nights. I'd been cooking for years, but the purity of this kind of cooking was so satisfying it was almost overwhelming. It really is an awesome feeling to be able to start a roast from a pig you raised, then saunter out to a row of crops to think about flavor profiles to pair with it. I think merely the ability to eat something you grew yourself is reason enough to start a farm. It's my dream, but to be able to do that and reach hundreds or thousands of people . . . that's like my wet dream.

The most rewarding thing about cooking once a week for the family was watching James, the son Heidi and her husband had adopted, eat. The kid had an appetite like nothing I'd ever seen, and I loved watching him stuff himself until his parents had to tell him to stop eating. Granted, he'd eat pretty much anything. One week, I made a kidney pie that Heidi's daughter, Wendy, unsurprisingly wouldn't touch. Despite her maturity on many other levels, she was not the most adventurous eater. James, on the other hand, struggled a bit with some learning disabilities, but he had the palate of Andrew Zimmern. This kid was more like me than he'll ever know. His predisposition for repeating patterns and his deep focus on meticulous tasks he'd set for himself will make him an incredible musician or cook someday. I'd often find James occupying his time by organizing intricate systems with his trucks. Within those systems were highly organized groups of rocks, trash, or scrap wood. We both enjoyed randomly breaking out in song and neither of us had much of a filter. Many times, when he'd say something deemed inappropriate, I'd be thinking the exact same thing.

James and I grew close over the course of our stay at the farm. He often called me his buddy, almost as if to reassure himself that we were friends. On some level he was a better friend to me than most I've had. He was completely unbiased and just knew that we liked a lot of the same things. He sat next to me at the dinner table, and I'd often catch him staring at my tattooed arms. He also had zero patience for watering the animals when it came time for chores.

I really valued the time I spent with James, and it was great to have someone younger actually look up to me, especially after everything that I'd gone through with my own father, and my feelings of regret about my son. But while I saw a lot of myself in James and hoped that he'd pursue whatever interested him, part of me couldn't help but hope that he'd just grow up and get a normal job. I wouldn't want anyone to be faced with the same temptations I was, and struggle the same way I did.

Every once in a while Heidi and her husband, Dan, would go out on a sort of date night. The kids would be at their grandparents, so Leigh and I had some much-needed alone time. If you aren't a parent, you don't realize how different your life becomes when you share every waking moment with two nine-year-olds. Usually, we would take the opportunity to plan for the future of Crux, and especially to test menu items that I was planning for upcoming dinners. One of said dinners was to be a collaboration with Kevin Sousa of Salt of the Earth in Pittsburgh, the restaurant we had visited on our way from Chicago to Maine. We had been in touch after eating at Salt, and he seemed keen on the idea of hosting Crux. The date had been set for late July, and we began planning the menu in June.

Kevin was a bit absent in the menu development phases, but he left me in the capable hands of Chad Townsend. After speaking over Skype once, I realized how in sync Chad and I were, and the rest of the menu planning went off without a hitch. I had grown oddly close with Chad after a handful of Skype sessions, so when he offered to have us stay with him at his home when we came in from Maine for the dinner, I agreed without batting an eyelash.

Honestly, having the Salt dinner on the horizon was probably what was keeping me sane after not having set foot in a restaurant kitchen in more than three months. It was the longest that I hadn't cooked in years. So when the family would leave us home alone, I took the opportunity to pull out all the stops and really go after some crazy concepts. We tested a dish with lamb tongue, avocado, soba, and cherry. I made soba noodles from scratch and deep-fried them (that needed some work; they turned out to have a consistency similar to those greasy crispy noodles they give you in a parchment bag at a Chinese take-out place). But the lamb tongue turned out great. I also tested a tomato dish with whey, soy, and jasmine which needed very little tweaking before being served to the guests at the Salt pop-up. We plated up some food for Heidi and the vegetable farmer, Cleetus, who couldn't seem to wrap their minds around the idea that people actually chose to eat like this. They were Mainers. And Mainers like their food simple and hearty.

Even though I loved the honest food that we cooked and ate on the farm, I was determined to find some like-minded people in Maine. With Portland being somewhat a food mecca, it turned out not to be that hard. Josh Potocki, the chef I'd met at the tattoo shop, introduced me to his friend, Joel Beauchamp, a very composed yet fabulous gay man who cohosted a local food show called *Food Coma TV* that was produced by Alex Steed and filmed by Kurt Graser. The premise of the show is that he and his cohost, the ever-exuberant, sometimes boisterous, and always entertaining Joe Ricchio, would head out to the far corners of Maine and sample local food and more often than not end up drinking copious amounts of booze.

Joel and Joe became great friends of ours and we often found ourselves heading into Portland to visit them, which could be unwise when we had work the next day and had to stumble through chores tired and hungover. Thankfully, we didn't have work the day after we joined Joel, Joe, and the crew of *Food Coma* in Old Orchard Beach. As my tattoo artist friend John Biswell told us, Old Orchard Beach is Maine's Jersey shore, but everyone is French-Canadian and smokes Virginia Slims.

He wasn't kidding. We drove down the main drag looking for parking, and we must have passed five middle-aged French-Canadian women wearing airbrushed T-shirts reading some shit like WHAT HAPPENS IN OOB STAYS IN OOB, smoking Virginia Slims, and hobbling drunkenly toward some overcrowded bar blaring club music. We had essentially arrived at my personal version of hell—wasted teenagers, bad tattoo parlors, busted old carnival rides grinding on ancient unoiled wheels.

When we finally spotted the *Food Coma* crew, they were seated outside a place called Hoss and Mary's and were filming some segment that should have been subtitled "Heart Attack Three Ways." We helped them polish off the dessert portion of their epic meal and headed to a bar, where we ate a few random plates of food that I chose to find acceptable as a stomach coater for the night of drinking to come. The night began to spin out of control when it was decided that we had to experience The Pier, a long strip of shops full of crap to ultimately lure tourists out to a nightclub. We had some shots at the god-awful place and were almost immediately accosted by a tattoo artist chick who knew me from Kylesa and apparently wanted to tattoo me and show the entire bar her tits. We tried to escape the bar unnoticed, but she and her drunk-ass friends chased us down the pier (I wish I were kidding) and nearly caught up with us as Joel and Joe were filming their closing statements for the episode. I don't remember everything from that night, but, thankfully, I will always have that episode of *Food Coma TV* to jog my memory.

A few years ago, that night would have seemed pretty fucking tame. And it certainly would have led to other things. But I'm proud to say that I really have reached a point where I can manage one crazy night every once in a while without suddenly bingeing on crack all over again.

Joe Ricchio, as it turned out, was good not only for ridiculous adventures in far-flung Maine towns, but also was the best guide to what was happening in the Portland food scene, which was pretty vibrant and bustling. It was with him that we had what were probably our two best meals in Maine—at Pai Men Miyaki and Bresca.

Pai Men Miyaki was particularly close to Joe's heart—he had worked for Chef Masa Miyaki—and he took us one night to experience the yakitori bar, which is what the restaurant became after five thirty P.M. We went straight to the bar, where we were greeted by smoking grills and cold beers. We had some appetizers, all of which were delicious, but Joe swore by the hamayaki, which I was a little skeptical about at first. My mind doesn't necessarily jump to truffle oil when pairing eel sauce, spicy mayo, crab, and scallop, but I have to say that shit worked.

We must have eaten the entire yakitori. We were presented with plates of skewered chicken parts (some of which—like the breast plate—weren't even on the menu) and beef tongue and pork intestines. This didn't faze me—as far as I'm concerned, the weirder the better. Tongue and intestines are my bread and butter. It was all fucking awesome, but the real shocker was that my favorite dish was the cihire, or dried skate wing, which they serve with spicy mayo designed to stand up to the sweetness of the dried skate. I was so enthusiastic about the meal that I left Pai Men scheming about opening my own yakitori place. Where Chef Miyaki's was elegant and clean, mine would be grungy, loud, and slightly obnoxious. To this day, I'm still revisiting it as a concept.

On our last night in Maine, before we headed to Pittsburgh for the Salt dinner, Joe set up a dinner for us at Bresca, which seemed to come recommended by everyone in Maine. And it was clear when we got there that they were ready to show us what they were all about. We ordered à la carte, but the kitchen snuck in some awesome courses that weren't on the menu, including every single pastry course offered. That didn't come as a total surprise to me—Chef Krista Kern Desjarlais is known for her considerable pastry experience. At the end of the night, I felt we'd experienced the best kind of Maine cooking. All the food there was simple and honest. There was nothing fussy about it, just like the rest of the state, but I could tell by looking at it how much thought went into each component of every dish.

Finally, we were ready to leave the farm and head to the big city—this time Pittsburgh—for our first Crux dinner in months. But before we did that, we decided that we'd make good on my previous threat of hiking the Appalachian Trail, or at least part of it. The first mile of the trail that we hiked was purely accidental. We didn't even know we were on the Appalachian Trail until we came across a trail marker. At first we thought it must be a mistake. The Appalachian Trail seemed so wild and so mythical in my mind that it wasn't possible we just happened upon it when we were driving from our rent-a-site campground to find a place to fish. But it was, and we had. I think Leigh could tell she was in trouble, because it dawned on me that we had to start hiking the trail immediately.

It wasn't an ideal time for me to be pacing out into the wilderness of Maine, with the Salt dinner to plan, but I needed to really let go of all outside influences and clear my head. I had left Chicago to come to Maine to stop, take a breath, and figure out what I wanted to do with my life. While some of that had crystallized during my time at the farm, it was so busy there that it hadn't given me all the time I needed.

I could tell that Leigh didn't want to hike, that she was looking deep inside herself for reasons it wasn't possible. "We have the car," she ventured. "Where would we park it?"

Unfortunately for her, we quickly found out that wherever the trail crosses a major road, there is almost always a parking area. Finally, she acquiesced and we set off to buy some real outdoorsy shit, like an axe and some campfire cooking equipment.

We spent almost a month on the trail, and though we weren't really outfitted with the right packs to carry all the crap we were lugging with us, we hiked a pretty respectable section, taking only one break in the middle of our trek to restock on food. This time around, though, we weren't just dumb city kids trying to pretend to know how to camp. We were better prepared to survive in the woods, though some things still don't make much sense to me. We had those tablet things you put in stream water to treat it, for example, but I think I used one once and then never thought about them again. The Appalachian Trail in Maine has a lot of rapidly flowing water and even some natural springs, so we figured to hell with it as long as Wylie wasn't taking a dump upstream from us.

We chose to enter the Appalachian Trail in a section we could easily bail from if something went terribly wrong. By that I mean, we didn't start our hike at the base of the highest peak in Maine. We kept it simple, and bought a trail guide so we could determine which area of the trail followed a river for the longest distance. We had the dog out on his first big outdoors adventure and I had no idea if Leigh would actually last two weeks on a trail without a shower.

We spent the first week living in an area about four miles off the entrance to the trail at Monson. Monson itself was a strange town. Its economy today is based largely on tourism and the Appalachian Trail. There were signs for boardinghouses, resupply points, and plenty of hunting stores, but absolutely no place to get camping gear. It took us almost an entire day of driving around to find a place that sold so much as a backpack. Even Chez Reny's (Renys is an independent mom-and-pop version of Walmart and a Maine institution) let us down this time.

When we finally found a backpack, I was cranky and paranoid that we wouldn't make it to a campsite before dark, but we camped right off the trail near the river. We spent the next week in one spot. It was like some sort of elven knoll out of *The Hobbit*. It was surrounded on three sides by water, and it was protected by trees on all sides. While I was looking to commune with nature, I wasn't trying to get eaten by it. Once I secured the perimeter, Navy SEAL–style, it was exactly what I was looking for to get my head together. I spent my days at the river fishing, and we spent our nights drinking whiskey, sitting by the fire, and cooking the trout I caught.

I went to the woods seeking introspection. I assumed this would take place during my waking hours—hiking the trail and staying in its least-touched frontier. However, in an effort to not force anything, my mind stayed blank. Most of my time was spent fishing, gathering wood, and foraging, using the little knowledge I have on the latter subject. This led my mind to wander freely after dusk.

In the woods, I started to dream as I never had before. Anyone who has spent time in the woods should know immediatcly what I speak of. These weren't pleasant dreams—there wasn't any flying or swimming through the air or fucking that girl I never had a chance with. But they were vivid as hell, borderline hallucinatory, mind-bending and complex. Every morning, I'd wake up and think about them as I baited my hook and rolled my Perique tobacco in Job 1.5's.

One dream in particular stands out: I was at a pop-up dinner, but I was a guest and not a cook. I looked to my left. There was my mom next to my grandmother and across from my grandfather, who looked rather lively and well, given that he's been dead since I was eighteen. The interior of the restaurant was chartreuse with walnut paneling draped around an open kitchen with four chefs just finishing up their mise en place for service. They were chefs Brad Farmerie from Public in NYC, Chris Curren from Blue 13, Dave Beran, and Curtis Duffy from Avenues, who are now at Grace in Chicago.

As soon as I did a second take at the line, Curren called me over. We'd had a problematic relationship in real life since the previous fall, when he'd made some pointed comments on Twitter about addiction. In my dream, he tried to explain those comments, and apologized. And he had a beard, a large, black beard. I returned to my seat, confused.

The next person to approach me was Beran, who came to

the table with a greeting not all that different from the greeting I've seen him give at Next. Except it ended with a hug. At this point, I knew that either I was in a dream or I had woken out of a coma only to be led directly to this event.

Finally, it was Curtis Duffy's turn, and he came bearing the first course. The Mochi Bomb. An orblike serving vessel with orblike indentations, holding "mochi" filled with sake. He punctured both sides of said "mochi" with a straw. He began to "shoot" with my mother. I looked down at my place setting, and there sat a heaping bowl of trout roe.

With a start, I opened my eyes. I wasn't in a restaurant, and my family wasn't there. It was three A.M., and I was in a cold, damp tent in the middle of the wilderness of Maine, on the shore of the Piscataquis River on the Appalachian Trail. None of it was real. It was all just a dream.

I thought about that dream a lot that day, and for many days to follow. And finally, I realized I was trying to pull some dramatically eloquent meaning out of nothing more than a random firing of synapses sparking a pictorial video behind my eyelids while I rested.

Mado was painted chartreuse. Tribute was floored with walnut. During my dinner at Avenues on one of Duffy's last nights, I was served raw alcohol in my dessert upon requesting the opposite. This was after Duffy had left for the evening, mind you. I still hold a grudge about what Curren tweeted at two A.M. that morning last fall. Beran's presence? He hired me, Achatz didn't. After my departure from Alinea, I've always sought his acceptance and approval. The trout roe seems simple enough: Slowly being digested inside me were six whole fish. Most important, I was never alive to see my mother, grandmother, and grandfather all in one place before his funeral.

What was Brad Farmerie's meaning? I have no fucking clue. But that was the piece to the puzzle that left me thinking this: Maybe everything isn't random. Maybe somewhere down the line, Brad will have some role in my life. To be honest, I'd forgotten about him after leaving NYC. Why would he make an appearance in a dream whose every aspect, other than him, I could trace back to a legitimate time in my life? Here's to you, Brad Farmerie. We've never met, but if that changes, you can be damn sure it'll mean something.

I stayed up the rest of that night by the river in Maine, thinking of all I'd gone through to get there. All the jobs, the girls, the binges, the intense periods of sobriety and work, all the dishes, all the chefs I'd known, all the places I'd lived. And there I'd landed, in one of the most beautiful places I'd ever been, feeling more at peace than I'd been in a long time. I was ready for the next step, wherever it would take me. And I'd like to think that the dream I had that night was giving me permission, just a little bit, to accept the past and remember that it would always be with me as I moved ahead.

They say a cat has nine lives. I couldn't tell you, sitting up in my tent that night, how many of them I'd burned through up to that point. But for the first time in a long time, I knew that now I was living them the right way, savoring them, and remembering to always land on my feet.

EPILOGUE

I've been called many things over the years—some good, some less so. But there's one thing that I think everyone in my life will agree on, from my biggest fans to my harshest critics: I never do anything the way people expect me to.

Most people aren't lucky enough to know before they're nine years old what they want to do with their lives. But for me, it was never really a question—my fate was sealed in the back of the Whistle Stop Café, chopping corn at my mother's counter. I was born to feed people, to have a restaurant of my own. And I'm proud to say that by the time this book comes out, I will be well on my way to doing exactly that. And that I did it in a way that no one expected.

I've dreamed about my restaurant for as long as I can remember, watching it morph from vision to vision as I jumped from job to job and city to city. Countless times, I thought that I knew what it would be like to have a place of my own,

that I had a specific direction that was calling me. And countless times, I changed my mind. Ironically, though, it wasn't
until I was able to let go of all of those expectations, to abandon the traditional path, to think on a level that was bigger
than just me and my experiences, that I was able to start to
make those dreams a reality.

I founded Crux in the aftermath of my Tribute disaster
because I didn't think that there was a place for me in the traditional culinary world; that if I wanted to cook without confines and boundaries, I'd have to eliminate them. To some
extent, I was right. Crux has given me the space and the freedom to grow as a cook on my own. But what I hadn't counted
on was the ways in which it helped me see that I wasn't actually on my own at all. Being a chef isn't a solitary pursuit—it
is communal, in the most profound sense of the word. That's
a lesson that I'll take with me for the rest of my career, and
especially for the next few months, as I finally break ground
on the dream that's been building for twenty years. And it's a
lesson that I'm not sure I would have learned, entirely, had I
not made one last, unexpected stop: Pittsburgh.

My time in Pittsburgh started with two pop-up dinners
that, symbolically, would come to embody much of what I
value as a chef and what I want for my restaurant. First, there
was the dinner at Salt of the Earth, the Kevin Sousa restaurant that we had visited on our way to Maine last spring. He
had invited us to Pittsburgh for a pop-up dinner, and we'd
spent much of our spare time at the farmhouse testing dishes,
planning a menu, and talking to Sousa and his team getting
ready for the dinner.

When the day finally came, it was exciting. Salt was, like wd~50 and Alinea, inspirational in its dedication to experimentation and new technique, and together, we were able to turn out some truly innovative food. We were spraying carrot juice into liquid nitrogen and pairing beet ice cream with Hungarian honey truffle, rose, granola, and white chocolate for fuck's sake. That night felt like a marathon—fourteen courses, with bites before and mignardises after. All hands were on deck, but even so, it felt like we pulled it off by the skin of our teeth. By the end of it, Sousa made it clear that I had a place at Salt, if I was ready to move on from Maine.

Leigh and I debated the merits of Pittsburgh—we had never anticipated landing there when we left Chicago, and she was still dedicated to completing our farm internship with Heidi. But I felt like we had learned all that we could from our experience there, and Heidi graciously agreed and let us go. Before we did, though, we had one final obligation in Maine—a Portland pop-up that we had planned with our friends Joel and Joe. I was anxious to get started with the next steps and with our new life in Pittsburgh, but it was important to honor the commitment, and as I started planning, I also saw how befitting it was as a final nod to our time there.

First, there was the camaraderie. It felt like everyone we had gotten to know in the Maine food world came to lend a hand, from Joe and Joel to my friend from the tattoo parlor, Josh Potocki. It was easy to work with people that I felt such a kinship with, all of us together doing what we loved. But the other important thing about the Portland dinner was what was missing—for the first time in as long as I could remember,

I kept things totally pure. No chemicals, no fancy equipment, and no more than two flavors per dish. Like cucumber and soy, or beet and oxalis. Every now and then we would insert an herb that was foraged by either myself or Jenna Rozelle, a forager I met in Maine, like evening primrose, sea blight, or sheep sorrel, for enhancement, but I really wanted to show that my food wasn't all smoke and mirrors, that I knew how to orchestrate a dish based off flavor that celebrated simplicity and not just complicated technique.

With memories of those two dinners in mind—one as experimental as anything I'd ever done, one as homespun and simple—I was ready to start the next chapter. Before I even started working in Pittsburgh, it became clear to me that the food community there was special. Leigh and I didn't have much money to spare; we'd been receiving only a small stipend from the farm, and we'd blown most of our savings staying in Portland for the pop-up. But almost immediately upon hearing that we were coming, a chef we'd met at the Salt pop-up offered to let us stay at his house until we got settled and found an apartment.

His name was Keith Fuller, and he was the owner of a restaurant called Root 174, and apparently, he was also our guardian angel. Our first full night in Pittsburgh, we all convened at his restaurant, and over simple, locally sourced fare, he introduced me around to his friends—all part of Pittsburgh's growing food scene. I've spent plenty of time with fellow chefs, and they're some of my favorite people, but they're also competitive as hell, gossipy, and even vindictive, especially in DC, New York, and Chicago, where I'd spent the bulk of my career. But I could tell that things in Pittsburgh were different, even on my first night in town.

Keith had literally opened his home to me, a fellow chef who could easily have become his direct competition, because he was genuinely excited about what I could bring to this burgeoning food scene. And he wasn't alone. Quickly, one of my favorite places became a spot called Bar Marco. The owners aren't exactly your typical restaurateurs—they're just a few dudes from Greensburg, Pennsylvania, who love eating and drinking and, above all, innovation. They've decided to let up to eleven pop-up businesses set up shop in and around their facilities free of charge, just as a tip of the hat to the idea of people doing what they want to do. There's an art gallery upstairs, a knife-making workshop in the basement, a juice bar on the sidewalk outside, an old Vietnamese woman making banh mi in traditional garb, and a parking lot full of food trucks.

When I first heard about what they were doing, I thought it had to be a joke—how could any self-respecting restaurant owner literally open their doors to the competition like that? But in a short amount of time, I came to respect the hell out of them. They care more about their community and how to progress the food scene than they do about the bottom line. I was proud to be a new member of that community, and want to take that same spirit with me to every next step I have in the future.

Eventually, Leigh and I found an apartment, and the night before we were about to move, Keith and I each had a rare night off, and decided to throw an impromptu BBQ. It was supposed to be simple and easy—burgers and dogs and that kind of thing. But a quick grocery run turned into a two-hour tour of Pittsburgh's wholesale facilities, and soon enough, we were churning out over thirty pounds of smoked and grilled meats. There was a fifteen-pound rib roast and six huge pork tenderloins, plus whey-poached, masa-crusted brussels sprouts, grilled watermelon salad, grilled squid with smoked potatoes, and Sriracha-deviled eggs. I've never felt so at home as I did that night. It's always been easiest for me to forge connections with people through food, and cooking with Keith that day, I knew that he got me on a meaningful level. It was our day off—the one day we should've been content to half-ass our way through some burgers—and we ended up essentially holding a pop-up BBQ dinner in our own backyard. Talk about taking your work home with you.

Unfortunately, things weren't going so well at my actual job. As planned, I had come to Pittsburgh to work with Kevin Sousa at Salt. I knew it was going to be a menial gig, and that was fine, because what I really needed was to pay the bills while I focused on Crux and on finally getting plans together for the grand finale—my restaurant. But pretty immediately, it became clear that Sousa and I had different ideas. My hours were long and difficult and the caliber of the cooks underneath management was low, but the last straw was the fact that he saw Crux as a conflict of interest and didn't want me hosting any events while I worked at Salt. It was an easy choice for me—Crux was almost exploding with offers, and potential partnerships, both in Pittsburgh and around the country. I felt like I still had a lot to learn from it, and that it was a part of my identity. I wasn't about to lose that for an hourly wage.

Leaving Salt was a pretty big blow at first—I had essentially uprooted my life to move to Pittsburgh and work there, and now I was stuck. Leigh had already found a job working in an art gallery, and while we hadn't moved yet, we'd signed a six-month lease on an apartment. I knew that I was going to be busy with Crux, but I also needed a way to pay rent for the next half a year. But, as they say, sometimes one door closes so another can open, and looking back on it, I couldn't be more thankful about the way things worked out.

Once again, Keith stepped in to save the day—not with a job, but with an invitation to a Labor Day gathering at an Italian restaurant on the South Side of Pittsburgh called Stagioni. The chef, Stephen Felder, came out to have some drinks with us, and we hit it off immediately. It was Labor Day weekend, and it seemed like we were all looking to let off some steam—I had just lost my job, and, as it turned out, Stephen had just lost one of his cooks. It didn't take long for the pieces to fit together, and by the end of the night, we were shaking hands, and I had a full-time gig at Stagioni.

After working at Salt for a few weeks, Stagioni felt like a breath of fresh air. Sousa had never wanted me to mention the restaurant on social media, and now my Twitter feed could once again stretch out its uncensored wings. Stephen encouraged me to tweet pictures of the food we were doing and things we were saying. And that was easy to do, because it was food that I believed in: simple, clean Italian food. Like many Pittsburgh chefs, Stephen is committed to fresh, locally sourced product, and the restaurant is very farm-centric, with a lot of canning, pickling, and curing. In Maine, I was reminded over and over again about how much beauty there is in simple, homegrown food, and I was impressed and immediately comfortable with Stagioni's commitment to that.

Perhaps even more important to me was Stephen's attitude toward Crux. Stephen encouraged and supported my every move with Crux, eventually even traveling with me to cook alongside me at some of our pop-ups. It was important to me that he understood what Crux and I were all about, both logistically, so that I could tailor my schedule at the restaurant around events that were happening, and also philosophically. I'd been working in restaurants for almost fifteen years, and knew how easy it was to get into a rut. The fact that Stephen seemed instinctively to understand what Crux was all about made it clear that he was going to be someone I could work with.

When I first started Crux, sitting in my ex-girlfriend's apartment in Chicago in May of 2011, broke and unemployed and fresh from rehab, I had a sort of fantasy of what it could become. Anyone could do a pop-up or two—but I had dreams of something much bigger than that, much bigger than I was. And, finally, after a year and a half of building, it seemed to be snowballing in a way that was making that fantasy a reality. Instead of me continually breathing life into Crux, it felt like it was starting to function—even thrive—on its own.

I'd come to Pittsburgh in part because so many local chefs had expressed interest in partnering with me to host Crux dinners. And over the next few months, we were able to host several Pittsburgh dinners, including one of my favorites, a "Dinner and a Movie" night, paired with *Amélie*, which sold out in under two minutes. But what was even more exciting was the offers that were starting to pour in from other places. During the fall and winter, Crux traveled to host dinners in New York City, Chicago, Miami, and a three-day marathon in Calgary, Canada, where we pulled off three dinners in three different restaurants.

In many ways, working with Crux had never felt more exciting than it did that fall. I was pushing the envelope in ways that I never had before, and cooking some of the most innovative, interesting, conceptual dishes. I had a particular connection to Calgary, an incredible food city with welcoming, adventurous people. Between dishes like morel cotton candy, pear dusted with cabbage, and a deconstructed Caesar salad with oysters, scallops, and kimchi, I made instant friends, and even sketched out plans for a standing-room-only yakitori bar for sometime in the future.

It was completely invigorating to work with Crux as I finally started to see it take off in the way I wanted it to, but it also became increasingly clear to me that it was time for me to move on with my career, and to pass the baton to someone else. I had learned a tremendous amount, and will always be proud of what I was able to build it into, but I also felt like I had accomplished my goal, and gotten what I needed out of it. And, of course, there was that same dream that had been tugging on me since I was nine years old. It was time to make that a reality.

There were a lot of factors that made it possible this year to start to think in a real way about having my own restaurant, but I can't emphasize enough how much of it I owe to Stephen Felder and to Stagioni. For years, I had been trying to envision starting my own restaurants while working in places that not only didn't feel like me, but also didn't entirely feel like the people who owned them. Stephen showed me how that could be different. He and his girlfriend live above the restaurant, and they've made it, in every sense of the word, an extension of their home. He has a garden out back, and a small, knowledgeable staff that feels like family. And he changes his menu almost every day, both to give him the opportunity to use the best possible product, and also to keep experimenting, to keep trying new flavors, to keep thinking in different ways about the food that he's serving. The fact that he has been able to achieve this perfect balance between clean, simple food and creative, innovative culinary thinking has inspired me to go back to the dream I've had since I was a kid. When I started Crux, I wasn't sure if I'd ever be able to go back to the idea of just one restaurant again. Now I know that I can, and I'm ready to try.

Not only have I been inspired watching Stephen run his own restaurant in a way that makes sense to me, but I also think that my time at Stagioni was a necessary last step before starting my restaurant in that it helped me think about commitment and working with others in a new way. I told Stephen when he hired me that I would work for six months, and when I leave, it will have been exactly that. After years of jumping from job to job and going back on my word, I realize how necessary it was to know that I was also very capable of keeping it. When I started Crux, I thought that I wanted to be independent, but looking back on it, I think I really did it so that I would learn to work with people, and finally, I think I have.

I started to think about everything I'd learned over the past few years—from Crux dinners, from the farm in Maine, and from Stagioni—and suddenly, things started to gel. I knew what kind of restaurant I wanted, one that reflected all of these things, and even more. And I knew what I had to do to start making it happen. After years of dreaming, and months of thinking, TMIP was born.

February, 2013, will mark six months at Stagioni and the end of our lease in Pittsburgh. TMIP is still in the early planning stages, but by that point, Leigh and I plan to have completed negotiations on a plot of farmland, likely in Michigan, and we'll move directly there and start building. The restaurant will be located on the farm, where Leigh and I will live, along with our staff, and grow and raise nearly everything we serve (the hope is that the only things we won't grow and raise ourselves are cattle, salt, butter, oil, and some spices and hydrocolloids). The dining model will be small and incredibly intimate, inspired by the model that we honed hosting Crux pop-ups, with a seating capacity of only fifteen diners.

There's an incredible amount to do in the next year. We need to start planting and purchasing animals, to renovate the house, and to begin construction on the restaurant. We plan to be done with construction by winter, 2013, and then will begin inviting people to the farm for what I envision as a series of soft openings—not too different from pop-up dinners, but with the knowledge that one day, they'll happen every day.

If I've taken one thing away from the past two years with Crux, though, it's that my best work is a product of all of my experiences, and I know that I still have so many places to travel, so many things to cook and to eat, and, effectively, so much to learn before I can have the restaurant that I want to have and that I know I can have. Before TMIP opens, I plan to go to North Africa to study primitive cooking methods, to return to Calgary to spend more time with some of the people I met while I was there, and, most important, to really dig into the Midwest to understand the land that we'll be building on, and especially its history—the foods that people have grown there, and the ways that people cooked it dating back to the Native Americans who inhabited it long before we did.

Opening a restaurant feels like both the beginning of a long road and the end of an even longer one. There were many points on that road where it seemed like a sick joke that I'd ever be able to start a restaurant—but the same could be said about writing a book, or even founding a successful culinary collective. I may not have done it the easy way, but I did it. And I know now that like Chris's original 6th Street Kitchen, like Heidi's kitchen in Maine, like Stephen's wonderful restaurant on the South Side of Pittsburgh, like the pop-up Crux dinners that I put on in Chicago and beyond, and even like the Whistle Stop Café in the back of a Jacksonville gay bar, TMIP will be my home. And I'll be ready to feed people there just as long as I can.

ACKNOWLEDGMENTS

In acknowledgment of the family, friends, and foe who have shaped my life, providing support and challenges. From the talented chefs willing to collaborate with me, to all those who made the documentation of the journey possible.

The writing team: Becca Shapiro, the team at Gotham, and Kari Stuart. The cooks: Keith Fuller, Joel Beauchamp, Josh Potocki, Chad Townsend, Domenic Branduzzi, Andrew Brochu, Corey Lyons, Jared Wentworth, Shin Thompson, Merlin Verrier, Luke Tobias, Kevin McMullen, Jaimee Vitolo, Dimitry Dinev, Zoe Feigenbaum, Brian Leth, Steve Newman, Jeremiah Bullfrog, Nicholas Wilkins, Dave Beran, Tom Pizzica, Nora Pouillon, Carlos, Stephen Felder, Andrew Hill, Dave Racicot, Justin Severino, Justin Steel, Cam Dobranski, Liana Robberecht, Jason McKay, Cleetus Friedman. The Friends: Aric Jackson, Pouya Asadi, Adam LaPalio, Veronika Kotlajic, Ehrrin Keenan, Katie Potocki, John Biswell,

Bar Marco Crew, Cara Delsignore, Harold Smith, Brett Hickman, Kris Olsen, James Miller, Scott Floyd, Joe Ricchio, Jenna Rozelle, Paige Jacoby, Simon Lamb, Michael Remsnyder, Trey Sanford, Skateboard, Melissa McCart, Lila Patil, Tim McNeela, Nelson, Lacie Garnes. The Family: Carline Vincent, Guy Eason RIP, Sydney Eason, Andrea Baltzley, Charles Marque, Brennan Marque, Lew Jenkins, Pam Jenkins, Mimi RIP, Scott Jenkins, Dottie Eason RIP, CM RIP, Janice Jinright, Jason Jinright, Tally and Jimbo Nail.